Memoirs
of a
Pakhtun
Immigrant

based on the memoirs of
Jamal Khan

and written by
Teresa Schapansky

enjoy!

Teresa

REVIEWERS SAY...

"A moving story of a Pakhtun immigrant to this wonderful country who remained steadfast to his objectives and through his hard work, dedication and sacrifice succeeded in providing a better future for his family.

It reflects the hard work of a person who left his home, in the remote mountains of northern Pakistan, in search of better opportunities and assimilated in an altogether different culture.

It's a story of triumph over difficult circumstances, highlighting the unlimited possibilities for those who demonstrate discipline and perseverance to their cause. It will be a rewarding experience for all who read it."

Mr. Tariq Azim Khan
High Commissioner for Pakistan, Ottawa

"5 STARS. A gripping and heart-warming tale starting with Gafoor, a Pakistani immigrant who came to Canada to find a better life for his wife and sons. The story starts in 1903, the year of his birth in his quiet mountain village. At the age of 18, eager to find work, he leaves his village and finds work on cargo ships, returning to his village between jobs. He marries a girl in the village, Basnoor. They have three sons.

In an effort to seek a better life, he finds his way to Canada in 1939 and jumps ship. He would be separated from Basnoor and his sons for many years as he sought to gain Canadian citizenship. By 1948 he has exhausted his efforts to become a landed immigrant and is ordered to leave the country. Sir Robert Holland, an attorney who had taken an interest in this kind, hard-working man, continues to intervene. Gafoor works hard to earn the money to sponsor his family - his eldest son would arrive in Canada first, eventually followed by his wife and sons.

The story flips back and forth between Canada and Pakistan. The second son, Jamal's journey to Canada is fascinating, first plane ride, first hotel, etc. How unnerving it must have been for him. The rest of the family followed, twenty years after Gafoor set foot in Canada.

The author has provided historical snippets in the chapters - Gandhi, Jinnah, WWII, the UK, the recognition of Pakistan as a nation etc., making the history come alive as it relates to the story. Schapansky has done a brilliant job with this memoir, a tribute to Jamal and his family. The photos at the end of the book bring it to life.

I read this in one sitting; it was engrossing, interesting and educational. A must read for any student and lover of history and memoirs."

Janice J. Richardson,
author of The Making of a Funeral Director

"Inspirational and quite absorbing, it brought to mind my own family history and my own immigration experiences in 1975 when I moved to the U.S.

Gafoor's life story is one of struggle and hope, it shows the greatness of Canada and its people, where it seems so natural for individuals to embrace complete strangers and assist them in their pursuit of a better life. This is not only a story of a Pakhtun immigrant, but also the story of the great heart of the Canadian people.

The inner strength of Gafoor in pursuit of his goals is quite unique and rare in the human condition; it says something about the upbringing of people like him, where the inner strength of the person far outweighs the drawbacks of literacy, culture, or immigration status. There is within such people a soul that sparkles, which draws people to them and allows them to move forward in life with hope and success, not unlike the ships he worked on which moved through miles of oceans to reach their destinations. A truly good read."

Raj Anand

"Highlighting the struggles of a family in search of a better life, this story revolves around the impoverished farming hamlet of Charuna, in the farthest highlands of Northern Pakistan, and the sawmill community of Youbou, on Vancouver Island, Canada, in the other corner of the world.

The hard working people living in both Charuna and Youbou are defined in direct contrast to the glitz and glamour described by the author, at the Metropole Hotel in Karachi, and the Empress Hotel in Victoria. The two entirely different social classes are portrayed, and give this story a distinct colour.

The author has chosen the common man as the subject of her research, while in sharp departure with the extant practice of blending in historical figures and celebrities. The projection of Pakhtun customs, hospitality, geography, historical glimpses, and the goodness of people such as Sir Robert Holland and the Bunker family make this an interesting read. The author has succeeded in her attempt at building bridges between and linking the two countries of Canada and Pakistan."

Muhammad Tariq
Consul General of Pakistan
Vancouver

"A very precise and chronological account that can be attributed to a dream of wanting future generations to know the struggles of life for the sole intent of that knowledge. Highly recommended."

J.P Willson, author of
Through the Mind's Eye: A Journey of Self-Discovery

"I highly recommend this memoir, which is rich in life-affirming tales of the kindness of strangers, during a time of separation and uncertainty for one family. Each chapter cleverly commences with some important historical events, which only enriches and puts into context the ever-changing historical backdrop."

Lucy Lang, author of
Dislocation-a moving story of a turbulent childhood

"Jamal Khan and Teresa Schapansky came together to tell a very important story; one of courage, adventure and the wish to make a family's life better. We must thank Jamal Khan for sharing his family's story and Teresa for the joy with which she wrote."

Elaine Fuhr, Freelance Reviewer

Disclaimer

This story is based on the personal accounts of
Jamal Khan, and has been created with only the most
honourable intentions.
Events have been depicted according to his
memories and are fact based to the best of
his belief and knowledge.

Further reading into historical facts that coincide with
the personal events described herein, can be found in
the bibliography located at the end of this book.
All website information is current
as of December, 2016.

Memoirs of a Pakhtun Immigrant
Copyright © 2016 Teresa Schapansky
All rights reserved.
The author may be reached at:
www.teresaschapansky.com

ISBN 13: 978-1-988024-07-3
ISBN 10: 1988024072

DEDICATION

by Jamal Khan

Nineteen-thirty-six was an exciting time. To name only a few notable events, *Gone with the Wind* was published, the construction of the Hoover Dam was completed, and the Summer Olympics were held in Berlin.

This was also the year that I was born.

As my story is being written, I am nearing my fiftieth year of marriage. I have been blessed with five children and nine grandchildren. I am incredibly proud of each of them. I will soon turn eighty years of age. These are my twilight years.

Family is the most important aspect of my life, and it is for this reason that this book exists.

We all need to know who we are, where we've come from, the struggles we've faced, the burdens we've carried, the joys we've experienced, and the lives we've lived.

It is my greatest wish that these pages become the legacy that I leave my loved ones - handed down throughout the generations.

My dear family, you are my greatest gift. This book is dedicated to you.

FROM THE AUTHOR

by Teresa Schapansky

In June of 2016, I received a message from a cherished high school friend. Polite folk that we are, he and I exchanged our usual pleasantries before he got down to business. His dad had been hoping to have his story written for quite some time, and he asked if I might be interested in taking on a project such as this. Would I ever.

Since then, I have met with Jamal 45 times, and each meeting, beginning and ending with a hug, has lasted anywhere from an hour to three hours. This book is the final product of those visits (and 90 hugs).

The original purpose for the writing of this book was to ensure that the history of how his family came to be in Canada would not become forgotten nor lost over time. Our aim was to chronicle times and events, woven from Jamal's memories, for his present and future family members to pass down throughout the generations. We agreed it would be helpful to add information at the beginning of most chapters to put the timeline into perspective concurrently with other events taking place in the world at the time.

Jamal and I were literally on the same page, when during the development phase, we realized that this story had the potential of being enjoyed globally. In both respects, I sincerely hope we've done it justice.

Throughout this project, Jamal and I have shared every single emotion. We've belly laughed, we've shed tears, and we've raised our fists in triumph. We've talked about our children, discussed theology, the local economy and the future of housing. We've touched on local politics as well as the political debate taking place in the United States. We've worried about the poor. Our conversations know no bounds.

A friendship that I will treasure forever has developed between us. When we get together, we don't notice the 35-year age gap, nor that our religious beliefs, gender and skin colour are not the same. We've simply become best friends for life.

I would like to thank Saleem for reaching out to me, and I'd like to thank Mrs. Khan for welcoming me into her home time and again, and for her wonderful hospitality. I also thank my new friend, Jamal for allowing me the honour of being part of this incredible journey. Researching and learning the history of this family, discovering how Gafoor happened to arrive in Canada so very long ago, and working side by side with Jamal has without a doubt, become one of the most personally rewarding experiences of my life.

Big thanks go out to my editors, Al Siebring and Dr. Muhammad Tariq (for their patience). Each of these gentlemen provided me with suggestions, edits and guidance and without their respective and unique contributions, this story would likely be sitting in my office, gathering dust for a long time to come.

Thank you to my family and friends for your nonstop unconditional love, support and encouragement. You are the fuel that drives me.

TABLE OF CONTENTS

Memoirs
of a
Pakhtun
Immigrant

based on the memoirs of
Jamal Khan

and written by
Teresa Schapansky

Library and Archives Canada Cataloguing in Publication

Schapansky, Teresa, 1971-, author
Memoirs of a Pakhtun immigrant / based on the memoirs of
Jamal Khan ; and written by Teresa Schapansky.

Includes bibliographical references.
ISBN 978-1-988024-07-3 (softcover)

1. Khan, Gafoor. 2. Khan, Jamal, 1936-. 3. Illegal aliens--Canada--Biography. 4. Immigrants--Canada--Biography. 5. East Indian Canadians--Biography. I. Title.

FC106.E2S34 2017   971'.004914110092
                          C2017-900533-2

1

GAFOOR

During the early 1900s, rapid advances were taking place in the areas of technology, industry, entertainment, and science, in the well known populated regions of the world.

For example, it was during this time that the first Nobel Prizes were awarded, the Wright Brothers flew their first airplane, and the Ford Model T was making its debut.

In the area of medicine, aspirin had just hit the market, Alzheimer's disease was identified for the first time, and insulin would soon be discovered.

As a result, everyday life for much of society would never be the same. However, there were areas of the world that remained untouched by the hands of time. One such place lay at the base of the Hindu Kush mountain range, just north and east of the Indus River.[12]

———

On May 15, 1903 in the remote village of Charuna,[3] in the North West Frontier Province[4] of undivided India, a child was born in a one-room house made of stone and clay. Although the family members of this child were poverty-stricken, they felt rich with knowledge; this knowledge stemmed from their customs and religious beliefs, which had spanned generations and survived the passing of time.

The moment this child's gender was determined, so was his destiny. It was expected that he would, as his father and ancestors before him had done, grow up strong, marry young, build a stone house, father children, and farm the land.

His birth was attended only by a midwife, who wasted no time summoning the messengers. Word spread fast throughout not only Charuna, but also the surrounding villages, that this family had been blessed with a male child.

The birth of a girl child would not have been celebrated as joyously; the reasons were practical, understood and accepted. For the lineage of each family to carry on, the strong arms and backs of the men were relied upon to lead and provide. Women, on the other hand, were cherished as child bearers, homemakers, and farmers, and they depended on men to look after them. This was the way it had always been.

The priest[5] arrived, proudly whispered the customary

call for the prayer of Azaan into the newborn's ears, and within the first seven days of his life, he was named.

As always, names were chosen carefully among the Pakhtun people, and he was called Gafoor. This was a strong, masculine title, which meant "forgiver" and "merciful".

Throughout the early years of his childhood, the boy would gather daily during the harvest seasons with his brothers, sisters, and other village children while the adults farmed the land. Never far from the watchful eyes of their parents, these children were content as they played, learned, and grew together, protected by the thick green canopies provided by the trees, and sheltered from the hot summer sun.

As dictated by tradition, once children - boys and girls alike - reached the age of ten, they would work the fields alongside their parents.

Gafoor's family was fortunate as their land was fertile, and this allowed them to harvest two crops each of corn and wheat per year.[6] Their bounty would not only sustain the family year-round, but it would also provide for their fellow villagers; those less fortunate who might find themselves in need.

This simple, yet laborious way of life lasted throughout his adolescent and teenaged years, and it might have continued into adulthood, if not for the interest he'd taken in the stories he'd heard about those who'd chosen to leave the mountains.

Widely talked about among the villagers, and held in high regard, were the brave men who had left the comfort and security of their mountain homes. These men for the most part, found work with shipping companies in Bombay, and rumour had it that this employment not only provided a good income, but also opportunities for traveling the world - a world which, for most of those left behind, could only be imagined in their minds' eye.

Gafoor listened to the stories and was growing into an idealist. He was eager to find out how much more the world might have to offer.

His desire to experience mysterious places firsthand, combined with his wish to learn about and meet new people, became more than he could bear. His dreams consumed his every thought, his curiosity grew, and he knew with certainty that he would not be satisfied living out his days in the remote village of Charuna.

One of Gafoor's older sisters lived in a nearby village, and he arranged to meet with her and her husband at their home. During the visit, he expressed his desire to find work with a shipping company. As luck would have it, he was speaking to the right people. The husband's brother had earned a prestigious position as an officer on a cargo ship, and he generously offered to speak to him on Gafoor's behalf.

Shortly after, Gafoor would meet with the officer. At first, the young man felt intimidated; the officer was the most powerful, and the biggest man he'd ever seen. This feeling of discomfort would be short-lived, however, as Gafoor was about to discover that this was also one of the nicest men he would ever meet.

As Gafoor was related to this man through marriage, he was assured employment. The officer wholeheartedly agreed to take Gafoor with him on his ship, but before that could happen, he would have to reach his eighteenth birthday. Gafoor would wait patiently for this time to come.

Not long after turning seventeen, Gafoor announced to his grandfather that he would be leaving home. His grandfather insisted that Gafoor tell his mother. She reacted much as he expected; she cried tears of sorrow when he told her his news. But Gafoor would not be swayed. He was adamant, his decision was solid, and he asked his family to pray for him. He would find his way to the better life he'd heard so much about, and he took his first determined steps away from the only home he'd ever known.

The clothes on his back were his only possessions as he began his lonesome journey by descending the seldom used, overgrown, zigzagged forest path that led out of his mountain village. One night, two days, and twelve tedious miles of walking through brush and bramble would pass before he would reach the nearest road that would eventually lead him to civilization.

Dishevelled, exhausted, dirty and hungry best described Gafoor's state when he arrived in Rawalpindi. This heavily populated metropolis was foreign to him, and he might as well have just arrived in an entirely different country. These people did not dress the same as the people of his village, and the scents and smells of food cooking differed greatly from what he was accustomed to.

Even though Gafoor felt shame over his unsightly appearance, he had no choice but to ask random townspeople for a loan. He requested only the bare minimum, a modest thirty rupees - this small amount would afford him the train fare to secure his passage to Bombay. Sadly, Gafoor was denied at each turn, and he then sought the homes of relatives to ask for help. They too, although always kind and sympathetic to his plight, turned him down. Feeling helpless and very much alone in the world, the young man sat down on a street corner, hung his head and began to cry. Through his tears, he watched as people passed by, and he wondered why he could not find a single soul willing to help.

His tears all but spent, Gafoor turned to face Mecca as best he could, dropped to his knees and prayed. Initially, he prayed for the health and well-being of the family he'd left behind, and then he prayed for himself. Although it felt to him as though an eternity had passed, it was not long before his faith was restored. With fresh strength and resolve, he returned to his feet and dusted himself off.

Gafoor thought long and hard about his remaining options. He recalled conversations he'd had with his father, and finally remembered - in detail - a story he'd been told. This particular story was about a man that his own father had helped many years before. To the best of his knowledge, this man lived in Rawalpindi. Gafoor knew his name, and began the onerous task of making inquiries. He now went in search of him - the one person who would surely be his last hope of reaching Bombay.

By early evening, just nearing dusk, Gafoor found the answer to his prayers.

When the man answered the knock at his door, he regarded the dirty, strange young man that stood on his stoop with suspicion and slight contempt. Once Gafoor introduced himself, and the man realized whose son this was that stood before him; he opened the door further and welcomed him with a heartfelt handshake.

Gafoor was invited to spend the night in this man's home. He had never before imagined how delighted he might be to see soap and a wash basin, and he eagerly rid his body of the filth and sweat that had accumulated from his days of travel. He then enjoyed a hearty meal with his new friend, and before each would settle in for the night, they discussed his dilemma while sharing a pot of tea.

The man did not agree to provide Gafoor with merely the cost of the train fare. Instead, he insisted on giving him fifty rupees, so that he could afford to eat while on his journey to Bombay.

The next day the men parted ways, in much the same fashion as when they had met. With a handshake, followed by a hug, and a promise of immediate repayment, Gafoor thanked him profusely, bade him farewell, and boarded the train.

His very first ride on the railroad would not be a glamorous one; it was stuffy and overcrowded, and he was not granted the luxury of a window seat. The train would creak, groan, lurch, and jerk incessantly for approximately fifteen hundred miles before reaching Gafoor's intended destination.

His journey had begun.

2

BOMBAY

At around the same time that Gafoor arrived in Bombay, George V, the grandson of Queen Victoria, and his wife Mary had been the Emperor and Empress of India for nearly ten years.

———

Five years earlier, Mohandas Karamchand Gandhi had made the decision to leave Africa to return to live in his native India. His attention at this time was focussed on making political waves to achieve the liberation of India, which had been under British Rule since 1858. By now, Gandhi's firm beliefs in non-violent solutions in the furtherance of civil rights and fair treatment for all had come to be regarded as acts of civil disobedience, and had led to his eighth arrest.[7]

It was now 1920, and by the time Gandhi's efforts would succeed, Gafoor would find himself halfway across the world.

———

Muhammad Ali Jinnah had been a member of the Indian National Congress since 1906,[8] had joined the All-India Muslim League in 1913, and was elected president of the latter organization just three years later. The dissimilar objectives that each of these political bodies followed had become apparent to Jinnah; he opposed the non-cooperation policy enforced by the Indian National Congress and resigned from this party in 1920.[9]

Though Jinnah believed in the eventual unification of India and in particular that the ongoing strife among the religions could be resolved, his primary goal was to represent the best interests of the Indian Muslims.[10]

Jinnah had come from humble beginnings - he was one of seven children, born on December 25, 1876. His ambitions were political; as such, he had chosen to study law and would become the youngest Indian to be called to the bar in England. Soon after, he returned to India and began his own practice, and at that time, was the only Muslim practicing law in Bombay.[11]

———

Canada helped found the League of Nations, a worldwide organization whose mandate was to promote peace.[12]   A succession of failures would lead to its replacement 26 years later - by the United Nations.

Canada's national police force, The Royal Canadian Mounted Police was established by the merging of the Royal Northwest Mounted Police and the Dominion Police.

———

In the United States of America, after decades of picketing, marching and lobbying, 1920 marked the year that women were at last granted the right to vote.

———

Patiently awaiting the arrival of Gafoor's transport in Bombay were three of his closest childhood friends. He climbed down from the train, his clothes grubby, tattered and far beyond repair, and searched for them through the crowds of people. Understandably, when at long last he spotted their smiling, familiar faces, he felt comforted.

The Pakhtun people abide by and follow an ancient, unwritten code of conduct known as Pakhtunwali. One of the rules is that of hospitality. While he had briefly experienced such warmth from his friend in Rawalpindi, Gafoor was about to learn just how closely each of these friends clung to their mutual heritage and traditional ways.

He was treated with the greatest of respect, and welcomed to their home where he was told, *Mailma de khuday milgaray day* - meaning, *a guest is God's friend.* Once he had eaten and had the opportunity to wash, he was led straight to the shop of a tailor, where he was measured for a new outfit. Gafoor's friends then provided him with fifty rupees, which was immediately sent by wire to his friend in Rawalpindi. Gafoor was relieved - his debt was repaid, and his new life was about to begin.

Gafoor moved into a shelter that was designed to temporarily support men while they were seeking work. There, he was given the basic necessities of life, and this allowed him the time required to pursue temporary employment and to explore. Everything was new to him - Bombay was heavily populated and bustling with nonstop activity. For the first time, he saw people of various cultures and races, from all parts of the world. Right in front of his very eyes, he observed the past and present collide - he bore witness to carts pulled by teams of oxen that had just as much right to travel the streets as did the recently introduced motorcars.

Gafoor soon turned eighteen and sent word of this milestone to the officer. Long before his allowed time at the shelter would run out, he would be working in the engine room of a cargo ship on its way to Germany.

Gafoor's excitement was beyond measure, and he adapted quickly to his new environment, which featured iron and steel and smelled of grease and grime.

He was trained as an oiler, and his primary responsibilities involved ensuring that the working parts of the equipment remained lubricated at all times. The importance of his duties was not lost on him - one small act of negligence or error on his part could cause the entire ship to stop running. The financial loss to the shipping company would be immeasurable and that, in turn, would likely cost him his job.

Taking great pride in his work, Gafoor would labour

steadily for four hours at a time, keeping busy with the oiling of the bearings in the engines, on the piston rods as well as the valve stems.

He was one of three oilers, and each would spell the other off after their respective shift was done. When eight hours passed, Gafoor would shower, rest and enjoy a meal before getting ready to return to the engine room where the cycle would begin again.

Much to Gafoor's delight, he encountered a familiar face on the ship - though at first he didn't realize who it was. His cousin, Sher Muhammad was working on the ship, and his job as a stoker was to ensure that the steam engines were constantly fed with coal. By the time each of his shifts were over, he would be so covered in soot that he was hardly recognizable. After that first chance meeting, Gafoor and Sher each made the arrangements with their superiors, and became bunkmates and better friends than ever before.

During his first voyage, Gafoor's ship crossed the Arabian Sea and entered the Gulf of Aden. It closely followed the coastline to the Red Sea, until it met with the Gulf of Suez. After a brief stint on each of the Nile and Damietta Branch Rivers, the ship continued its course, sailing through the Mediterranean and Alboran Seas, the Strait of Gibraltar, the North Atlantic Ocean, the Bay of Biscay, the English Channel, and finally the North Sea before reaching port in Germany.

Along the way, the ship stopped at various ports where it would refuel, as well as deliver and pick up goods of all kinds. The crew, when not on shift in the engine room, was often assigned the task of assisting with the unloading and loading of these goods, which were crated and labeled; each label indicating contents and destination.

Not all of the crewmembers were literate, and they depended on those that could read for direction. Like Gafoor, many had come from areas which were so isolated that education of any sort had never been an option.

Life on the vessel, to say the least, exceeded any and all of the expectations; true or misconceived, that Gafoor may have had prior to leaving his mountain village. The bunkrooms, though cramped, were kept spotless, and each person respected the other's personal space and privacy. Meals, abundant in variety, were provided in generous portions; no one left the dining room hungry.

When given the time and opportunity, he would venture up to the deck, sometimes alone, and other times with friends he'd made among the engine room crew. He enjoyed seeing and listening to the crash of the waves as they battered against the ship, and he fully believed that he'd never tire of watching the bow as it effortlessly parted the waters while they continuously moved forward.

Every so often, the ship's stay at port would be extended for a variety of reasons, and during these times, the men - once their tasks had been completed - were allowed onshore. Strict instructions were given and followed; they were ordered to stay within their groups, behave as ambassadors of the ship, and return to the ship on time.

Gafoor's first sailing lasted eight months from start to finish. When they arrived back at the port in Bombay, the Chief Engineer gathered all hands on deck, where they were verbally given the date as to when they would be expected to return, as well as the basic itinerary for their next scheduled trip. At this time, they were each provided with three months' leaves of absence in writing and payment in British coin for jobs well done. By the time Gafoor's feet once again touched Indian soil, he was no longer simply the child of a poor farmer; instead, he returned to his homeland a little taller, a little stronger, and most importantly, a knowledgeable and proud able-bodied seaman.

Before returning to the railway station, Gafoor visited his three friends and paid back his loan of fifty rupees, as well as the cost of the new clothes they had bought for him. Completely debt free now and with a clear conscience, he boarded the train to Rawalpindi.

He was greeted with a hero's welcome by the time he arrived home, and he knew that he had succeeded in joining the ranks of the village men that were held in high regard.

During his time off, Gafoor naturally slipped back into his peaceful, idyllic way of life. He had recently spent the better part of a year listening to the clanging of metal parts and the constant rumble of the ship's engines, but now he paid more attention to (and deeply appreciated) the sounds made by the children playing, the mumbling of the water buffalo and the wind whistling through the trees.

He would spend these months helping his parents with the farming of the land, and he saw the beautiful wonders of his countryside from a brand new perspective.

With Gafoor's financial assistance, his family's entire standard of living greatly improved. New cloth was purchased, and the tailor from a nearby village was summoned. He arrived, sewing machine strapped to his back, set up near the house, and spent days carefully measuring, cutting and sewing new articles of clothing for Gafoor's parents, brothers, and sisters. They would no longer go without.

3

BASNOOR

By 1932, the United States had suffered through the Great Depression for three years, and would continue to do so until 1939. Despite these tough economic times, the III Olympic Winter Games took place during the early part of February, in Lake Placid, New York, and the III Olympic Summer Games followed months later, in Los Angeles, California.

———

During May of 1932, violent rioting between the Muslims and Hindus in the City of Bombay, India, left thousands of people dead or wounded.[13]

———

Gandhi was arrested yet again, this time at his home in Manibhuwan, India. Only two years prior, he had led what eventually amounted to thousands of people on the Salt March, also known as the Dandi March, which began at his home, at Sabarmanti Ashram, and ended at the Arabian Sea. This well-organized and peaceful march was structured to directly defy the British monopolization of the production, importation and exportation of salt; thereby crippling the livelihood that for many, had been relied upon for generations. [14]

———

Gafoor would sail the seas for another six years, and he'd have the privilege of visiting countries all over the world. The duration of each trip would vary just as much as his visits home would - at times a whole year at sea might pass, and other sailings could last for as little as three months.

During his thirteenth year on the cargo ship, he was returning to Bombay with another load when he received a telegram from his village; this was the message he'd been patiently awaiting for some time. It stated that Basnoor, the bride his parents had carefully chosen for him years before, was now of age, and that upon his return home in 1933 he could expect to become a married man.

After their initial introduction and subsequent engagement had taken place, Gafoor couldn't help but notice that Basnoor would go out of her way to avoid him. She would look down, look away, and often cover her face in passing, fervently avoiding any possibility of eye contact. This was not unusual behaviour for a promised girl and it only served to heighten his level of fondness toward her.

Basnoor belonged to a family of good standing, and she was the only daughter born of eight siblings. Unfortunately her mother had died of illness when she was a young child, and their widowed father raised her and her brothers well.

Upon reaching the dock at Bombay, Gafoor's heart beat rapidly in his chest as he anticipated his big day. In keeping with Pakhtun custom, he knew that his bride would be kept far from him until the moment of their union. Now that the time was near, he was eager to set his eyes upon her; the young lady that was to become the mother to his children and his eventual lifelong companion.

At long last, Gafoor arrived home carrying two large suitcases full of exquisite new clothes for the event. He gifted each member of his family with such finery that they'd never before had the pleasure of wearing, and for Basnoor he'd chosen an elegant wedding dress of red silk, with an embroidered veil to match.

The entire village, as well as visitors from neighbouring communities participated in the day-long festivities, for a wedding was considered the most sacred of all occasions. The atmosphere was jubilant as the men gathered and shot their guns into the air, while village ladies - old and young - including female friends and relatives, assembled in Basnoor's father's home. Their hands were dyed with henna[15] for the event, and they spent hours singing wedding songs[16], playing tambourines[17], dancing, and often playfully teasing the bashful young bride.

Hours later, the guns were set aside and a brief wave

of silence fell over the people. Gafoor had never been happier, as his bride-to-be was carried in a carriage[18], decorated and draped with red cloth, which rested upon the shoulders of family members, toward his home. Musical instruments[19] continued to play in the background as the procession moved forward.

Even though her face was completely veiled, Gafoor felt certain that Basnoor would be the most beautiful woman he'd ever had the privilege of laying eyes on. She sat gracefully in the middle of the carriage, with her head bowed low when he gently reached toward her, and offered her his hand. She accepted modestly, rose and stood by his side.

Members of the two families gathered in front of the priest while a close relative - chosen to act as intermediary - conversed with Basnoor and Gafoor, to seek their respective consents to the union. A dowry was agreed upon and prayers were spoken by the priest, before Gafoor's mother stepped forward to whisper her blessings into Basnoor's ears. Side by side, the couple knelt in front of him to exchange their vows and garlands, and soon after, Gafoor and Basnoor were pronounced man and wife. Everyone rejoiced as sweets were generously distributed among the people. Their wedding celebration lasted well into the night.

The newly wedded couple would live with Gafoor's parents until they could afford to build their own house. Basnoor stepped gracefully into her new role as a married woman, and her husband's family treated her as they would treat one of their own.

On the third day after the ceremony, Basnoor returned to her childhood home, to join her female friends and relatives to help her family prepare the ghunsahey and darwesh[20], which would be placed in a special box for her to present to Gafoor's parents, upon her return to their home four days later.

Only two weeks after the wedding, Gafoor's leave of absence was cut short and, although he was heartbroken and reluctant to leave his new bride, he had no choice but to return to Bombay.

By the end of their first year of marriage, Basnoor had given birth to their first child, and two years later, a second child arrived.

For many years, their sons would experience the same sort of childhood that Gafoor had. They would gather daily during the harvest seasons with the rest of the children, while their mother and the other adults farmed the land.

Gafoor's routine would remain the same - while he worked hard to provide enough income to ensure that they hovered above the poverty line, he, Basnoor and their two children still shared his parents' home. Increasingly, he realized that he was unable to put to rest his ambitions to provide a better life for his loved ones.

Gafoor was finding it more and more difficult to leave for the ship as time wore on, and he just knew that somewhere and somehow, there had to be a way to earn a good living, without having to be separated from his family and home for months on end.

While at sea, Gafoor would listen intently to the talk among the crew, paying keen attention to those men that were more educated and well traveled than others. He'd overheard conversations about the United States of America, and this caught his interest; however, he'd recently overheard discussions that would last for hours, about yet another faraway and seldom heard of country called Canada. He'd not yet sailed to either place, but as Gafoor understood it, Canada was most promising; the ideal true north, strong and free. Privately, he now turned his thoughts toward finding a way to reach it.

4

CANADA

In July of 1939, Gandhi penned a letter to Adolf Hitler, the Chancellor of Germany, in essence asking him to avoid going to war for the sake of humanity. For reasons unknown, the letter was intercepted by the British, and never reached its recipient.[21]

———

Germany began the invasion of Poland in the fall of 1939. This event triggered the beginning of the Second World War, which was to become the most widespread conflict in history. Before its end, more than 30 countries would be involved, and over 60 million people would perish.

———

Lord Linlithgow, the viceroy for Britain - without having first discussed the matter with India - revealed that India would be joining the British in the war effort against Germany.[22] India reacted with mass protests - each member of the Indian National Congress party - the most dominant political party in India at that time[23] - put forth their resignations. In his role as president of the Muslim League, Jinnah subsequently requested that December 22, 1939 be known and recognized as the "Day of Deliverance" to celebrate those resignations.[24]

Ripple effects of the war were being felt across the globe, and all industries were affected in one way or another. One example of this was the shipping industry; typically harmless ships that had been built for the purpose of transporting passengers and the importing and exporting of goods would now be commissioned and converted by the military for battle use.

The cargo and passenger ship, *SS Rajputana*, built in 1925 and known for having carried celebrities the likes of Lawrence of Arabia, as well as Gandhi, would become one such ship. In December of 1939, after reaching port in Esquimalt, British Columbia, it would be renamed the *HMS Rajputana*, and fitted for combat. In the spring of 1941 this vessel, like many others, would fall victim to a torpedo assault and sink off the coast of Iceland.[25]

At this time, the Indian army consisted of more than

200,000 men, and it would soon grow to become the largest all-volunteer military unit known to man.

———

Gafoor enjoyed his leave of absence from the ship, and just as he had done for the previous eighteen years, took great pleasure in being home with his family and helping with the farming of the land. By the time he prepared to leave the village to head back to work, his sons were two and four years old, and he and Basnoor were expecting their third child.

Gafoor hugged his parents, his wife, and his children goodbye, and began the long journey. He walked away from his mountain village, down the now well-trodden path to the valley below. Miles later, he reached the road that would lead him to Rawalpindi. From there, he rode the train to Bombay.

Neither Gafoor nor his family had any way of knowing that they would not see each other again, for many, many years to come.

Months later, the ship returned to Bombay, and after unloading, the crew was informed that the next ship to leave, the SS *Rajputana,* would be bound for Canada. Gafoor was taken back, and he was not prepared for this. He knew that he had a quick decision to make, as this was his first opportunity, and very likely the last chance he'd have, to reach the land of freedom. Ultimately, he did not spend this time off by going home to his village, but instead, immediately signed up to join the next sailing. Gafoor kept his true intentions to himself, as he made arrangements to stay with the officer that had first provided him with his job, until the ship was ready to leave.

On Tuesday, November 7th, 1939, after many stops along the way and having travelled nearly 16,000 nautical miles, Gafoor's ship neared the southern end of Vancouver Island, on Canada's west coast. The helmsman steered into the Strait of Juan de Fuca, and finally the anchor was dropped at Esquimalt harbour. It took the crew two days to unload the cargo, and because new goods to load would not arrive until the following week, each of the crewmembers were granted a pass that allowed them to go onshore. All of the men showered and then dressed in their finest clothes before disembarking. Gafoor changed into his one and only suit, put on his hat and his long coat, and with only four dollars to his name, filed in line with the rest of the crew and left the ship.

Endless grey clouds covered the sky, and there was a constant drizzle of sleet. Despite the chill, spirits were high as the crewmembers talked among themselves, all the while exploring the streets of Esquimalt.

Gafoor felt pangs of guilt and torment by the time he reached his final conclusion; that in order to provide a better life for his family, he could not possibly return to the ship with the crew. What he was about to do was in direct contrast to his beliefs, and he hoped and prayed that the decision he'd made, would be the right one.

Not knowing the fate that awaited him, Gafoor slipped away from the others unnoticed, and headed toward the Johnson Street Bridge. His pace quickened as he crossed it, and he didn't dare look back.

In a matter of minutes, Gafoor had risked everything he'd known and loved, and had become an illegal immigrant in a foreign country. If he were caught, he was certain that he'd either face deportation or find himself looking out through the bars of a jail cell for any number of years. He would never be able to live down the shame.

His first order of business would be to try to locate people that shared his culture or language, and once he'd made those connections, he'd search for employment.

The sleet had turned to rain, and dusk had set in as he walked off the bridge and kept to the sidewalk, head down, and steadily moving forward. Unbeknownst to him, he had now entered the city of Victoria.

Several hours went by before a black automobile slowed down and followed Gafoor for a short distance before pulling up to a stop beside him. The driver rolled down his window and called out to him. Gafoor was weary, though cautious, as he approached the car, and to his great relief, he could plainly see that this man was of East Indian descent. Gafoor couldn't ever recall being happier to meet anyone than he was at that moment.

This driver had noticed Gafoor while he walked, and he instinctively knew that this was a man from India who was in need of some assistance. Kartar Singh kindly introduced himself, and then generously invited Gafoor to join him in his car. Gafoor accepted this offer with much gratitude, and he rode with him, far away from the city to the rural town of Paldi.

Paldi, a sawmill-based town set in a heavily wooded area located in the Cowichan Valley, was established in the early 1900s by Mayo Singh Manhas, who had immigrated years before, from a village of the same name, in Punjab, India.[26] Mayo, an experienced lumberman, welcomed everyone, regardless of race or ethnicity, that was willing to put in a long day's work, to become a member of the community. Gafoor was offered a job at the mill, and he moved directly into one of the bunkhouses. He would begin working on the green chain the very next day.

The green chain was the starting point for all new mill workers; it was here that the not-yet-seasoned planks would be pulled and graded, then sorted according to size. Gafoor learned quickly, and he was a hard worker. Before long, he would earn the number one spot at the sorting table.

Although Gafoor found this new line of work heavy, repetitive and exhausting, he was grateful for it. The lengthy, busy days helped to keep his mind away from missing his family. While the forest and fauna differed from that in Charuna, he found the climate similar and in this way, it felt like home.

The sawmill did not run on Sundays, and the men would often spend time together in the lunchroom, exchanging stories. As always, Gafoor would pay close attention to the talk from the more experienced men, and in doing so, he learned about a larger sawmill, owned by British Columbia Forest Products, that was located only a short distance away. By now he'd been working steadily at the Paldi mill for three months, and little by little, he watched as his savings had begun to grow.

Gafoor decided to investigate further, for he had to know whether or not greater opportunities existed for him. He caught the bus and took it to Youbou, another scenic, sawmill-based community, situated on the north shores of Cowichan Lake. Upon his arrival there, he had no trouble finding the sawmill on the outskirts of town, and based on the colour of his skin, he was immediately directed to the East Indian bunkhouse.

There, Gafoor discovered that the majority of the

workmen were followers of the Sikh religion. He was relieved to learn that though the conflicts between his fellow Muslims and the Sikhs continued to rage in India, he was welcomed, and there was no discrimination in the bunkhouse. The workmen all shared similar histories and experiences, and they were eager to learn about this newcomer, and how he had happened to arrive in Canada. Gafoor readily explained his situation. The friendly bunkhouse cook introduced him to the superintendent, Mr. Whittaker, who made a point of stopping in to visit with the workers each Sunday. Mr. Whittaker wasted no time in offering Gafoor full-time work. The very next day, Gafoor gave his notice at the Paldi sawmill, moved into the bunkhouse in Youbou, and began working on the green chain there.

The bunkhouse cook, a kind-hearted man of the Sikh faith, immediately began to prepare meals to set aside especially for Gafoor on the days when he would ordinarily serve pork. He was aware that the Muslim people could not consume such meats and it was not in his nature to allow any man to leave his kitchen without first having enjoyed a substantial meal.

5

IMMIGRATION

By 1940 two immigration-affecting regulations enacted by the Canadian Government had been in place for thirty-two years. The first, a continuous journey rule, meant that those wishing to migrate to Canada must have traveled non-stop from their native country. This proved impossible for Asian people. The second rule stated that immigrants originating from Asia must hold a minimum of two hundred dollars in their possession; this was unmanageable for most.[27]

These laws resulted in a dramatic decrease of new immigrants, and it meant that the previously landed immigrants, approximately 5,100 of which were of East Indian descent, would be separated from their families for undeterminable lengths of time.

———

The population of Canada in 1940 amounted to 11.3 million people, and of this number, nearly one tenth (1.1 million) served in the Second World War. On the home front, civilians in general would work longer hours to keep up, and women took on much of the work, including factory and assembly line positions, that men had historically been responsible for.

———

It was due to the persistence of Jinnah, and by his hand that the Lahore Resolution[28], which called for the division of India into separate states, and written by Sir Muhammad Zafrulla Khan, was passed.[29]

Although the name of the proposed new state, *Pakistan*, had been penned years prior by Cambridge University graduate and founder of the Pakistan National Movement, Chaudhry Rehmat Ali in 1933[30], it was not until after the passing of the resolution, that it became widely used.

Due to his ongoing efforts, Jinnah would, in a few short years to come, carve his name in history and become known in Pakistan, as the *Quaid I-Azam* meaning, *Great Leader*, the Father of the Nation, and the Founder of Pakistan.

———

During the early morning hours of December 7, 1941 the Japanese military launched a surprise attack on Pearl Harbor, the United States naval base located in Honolulu, Hawaii. The death toll including civilians and military personnel reached 2,403 and the wounded amounted to 1,178. The United States declared war on Japan the very next day.[31]

———

Back in Charuna, life without Gafoor had to carry on. For him to simply not return home during a leave of absence was completely out of character, and his family desperately worried about him. Three months after Gafoor had left, Basnoor had given birth to their third son. He'd been away for well over a year now. His family and friends had no way of knowing whether he was alive or dead.

The villagers were hardly discreet with their speculations as to what might have become of the young man who had been - until recently - held in high regard. While his family did their best to ignore the idle gossip, they could not deny his absence, nor the lack of his income. They adjusted accordingly and farmed more land to adapt and overcome the financial hardships. It would prove to be a struggle; however Basnoor and Gafoor's parents joined forces more than ever before, and persevered to make ends meet.

Across the world, in the little town of Youbou, Gafoor had established a solid reputation as an honourable, working man. Not once would he miss a day of work, and his tasks were all well done. He got along favourably with his fellow mill workers and earned the respect of his peers and foreman. He was at long last in a position to send word of his safety and whereabouts home, along with most of his hard earned savings.

Gafoor was acutely aware that employees of the

Department of Immigration randomly made their rounds from sawmill to sawmill, looking for anyone that might be working illegally. He was taken by surprise however, when immigration officers began to pay visits to the Youbou sawmill and direct inquiries were made about him. He never would discover how, of all the men working illegally, it was his name that appeared on their radar.

The foreman had become quite adept at not disclosing Gafoor's whereabouts when the immigration officers would present themselves unannounced. He had no hesitation in denying that Gafoor was there, when in fact he was. To protect Gafoor even further, the foreman strongly urged him to use another name on paper, and so for a while, Gafoor would sign his time cards under the alias of John Mohammed. Gafoor had more than proven his worth on the crew, and the foreman was prepared to go to great lengths to avoid losing this highly valued employee. In the end, these steps would be of no avail. Visits to the sawmill by the immigration officers only became more frequent.

Despite the fact that Gafoor had the friendship and full support of his peers, the fear and constant threat of deportation did not lessen, and became so overwhelming that he felt the need to run. With the approval of his foreman, and on the advice of his co-workers who had all pitched in to provide him with pocket money, he packed his few belongings and rode the bus to Victoria. He took the ferry to the mainland and then hailed a taxicab, which drove him to the railway station. He purchased a one-way ticket and was soon on the train heading east across the Canadian Rockies, bound for Edmonton, Alberta.

Following his arrival in Edmonton, the first person

Gafoor met and spoke with was a friendly, uniformed police officer. This gentleman was most helpful, and upon learning that Gafoor was seeking work at a sawmill, he suggested that he make his way north, a distance of nearly 100 miles, to the well-known lumber community of Chisholm. Gafoor immediately bought a bus ticket and was on the road again.

Gafoor truly felt that his prayers had been answered when he was welcomed to join the green chain crew and began working immediately. He soon discovered that he could not possibly have been more wrong.

Sadly, a lunchroom was not available for non-white people, and this resulted in quiet and lonely meal times, as he had no option but to eat alone. Furthermore, no accommodations existed for people of any colour. Even if rooms had been available, the very idea of a man of Gafoor's culture sharing lodging with white people would have been absurd.

The sawmill was experiencing a shortage of workers, and so the foreman kindly suggested to Gafoor that he dig a hole deep in the ground to sleep in. Gafoor did as he was told, and he was generously provided with bedding. It was wintertime, and the temperatures, more often than not, dipped well below the freezing point. By the end of his seventh day in Chisholm, Gafoor had become seriously ill with fever and soon developed pneumonia.

The substandard living conditions and his life-threatening illness made his mind up for him - as soon as he was well enough to travel, he would make the necessary arrangements to go back to Youbou.

Open arms welcomed Gafoor when he returned to the East Indian bunkhouse, and he was equally happy to be home. His co-workers had wonderful news for him, and he was promptly informed about an upcoming immigration meeting that was about to take place at the Empress Hotel in Victoria. Dr. Durai Pal Pandia, a prominent Indian lawyer who practiced in Vancouver, had recently succeeded in obtaining landed status for more than three hundred illegal immigrants, and was scheduled to be in attendance at this meeting. Gafoor was tired of falsifying documents, running, hiding, and constantly looking over his shoulder to avoid detection, and he immediately made plans to be at that meeting. He polished and stepped into his best pair of shoes, and wore his suit, hat and long coat. Deliberately dressed to impress, he caught the bus from Youbou to Victoria.

Gafoor had never before stepped foot inside a building as grand as the Empress Hotel, and he was awestruck by its elegance. He located the meeting room, and joined the line-up of hundreds of other hopeful men who shared his ambitions. They were all in the same predicament; they were simply looking for a way to legally live and work in Canada.

Gafoor's long wait in line finally came to an end, and it was his turn to speak with the lawyer. He did his best to remain optimistic as he approached the desk, introduced himself, and carefully explained his situation. Dr. Pandia, in turn, described his position, and unfortunately for Gafoor, the current priority was to assist members of the Sikh community, and not those of the Pakhtun heritage.

Even though personally he would not be able to help, Dr. Pandia agreed that Gafoor should apply to the Canadian Government so that he could remain in Canada legally. He clearly understood and sympathized with the difficulties Gafoor faced, and pointed him in the direction of his distinguished colleague.

Gafoor's first introduction to Sir Robert Erskine Holland later that day would develop into an unlikely friendship that would carry on throughout their respective lifetimes.

This heavily decorated man had retired from military service as a lieutenant-colonel, and had traveled across the world before choosing to call Victoria his home. Not only was he well versed in courts of law worldwide, but he had also held high government positions throughout Asia and the United Kingdom. Additionally, this gentleman had longstanding personal relationships with and access to a multitude of political offices and organizations. He would not sit idle during what should have been his retirement years; instead, he chose to spend his time and efforts to assist those that he deemed needed it most.

Sir Robert Holland had held office as chief commissioner for the North-Western Indian Province of Ajmer-Merwara from 1919 until 1925, and during the course of his experience there, had developed a soft spot for the Pakhtun people as well as a deep love for their culture. Upon learning that Gafoor was Pakhtun, he wished to speak with him privately. To this end, he handed a piece of paper to Gafoor, upon which he'd written his personal contact information and home address. Gafoor was instructed to attend at his residence the very next day.

Charitable by nature, Sir Robert Holland enthusiastically agreed to take up Gafoor's cause, and told him that it was time that he stopped running. He would spend the next eight years working diligently on his behalf.

In the meantime, Gafoor's superintendent at the sawmill took matters into his own hands, and wrote a letter to Mr. Taylor, the District Superintendent of the Immigration Branch, dated January 30, 1940:

"Dear Sir:

John Mohhamed has worked for this Company and its predecessor, Industrial Timber Mills Limited, during the greater part of the last eight years, and is at present in our employ.

We regard him as a valuable employee, he being a hard worker and skillful in his duties. He is a teetotaler and a non-smoker, and we understand, a man of some means.

Anything that you can do to regularize his status so that he can continue to reside in this Country will be appreciated.[32] "

Even though there is no record of any acknowledgment to this letter, it could only have had a positive effect toward Gafoor's ongoing efforts to remain in Canada.

6

CHARUNA

1945 welcomed the surrender of the German forces, which led to the long-awaited conclusion of the Second World War. Global struggles and suffering were far from over and it would take several years, even decades, for many countries to begin to recover from the overwhelming human and financial losses.

———

The United Nations was created.[33] This worldwide organization upholds the foremost objective of preserving peace and maintaining international cooperation to this day. The United Nations Charter was agreed to and signed by representatives from 50 countries - including those from Canada and India. The

United Nations took the place of the League of Nations, which was formed primarily for the same purpose after the First World War, but had proven ineffective in the prevention of conflicts, including the devastating Second World War.

——

In 1946 the Muslim League, led by Jinnah, won the majority vote to create Pakistan as an independent state. While Jinnah and Gandhi agreed on the liberation of India from British Rule, Gandhi remained adamantly opposed to the separation of Pakistan from India.

——

Jinnah and Gandhi each shared common, humble beginnings in their early, pre-political days and both had later pursued political careers. However, the visions each had for the future of India could not have differed more. Jinnah firmly believed that it would be in the best interests of the Muslim population to separate entirely from the Hindu and Sikh peoples.

——

The first telegram Basnoor received from her husband was delivered by a messenger, more than a year after he'd left India. She held it tightly in her fist, and prayed that it contained good news. She bundled up her three sons, set the youngest on her hip, and together they walked down the valley to a neighbouring village.

Once there, they visited the home of Saadullah Khan. Saadullah was the son of an officer that had served in Burma during the First World War. By all accounts and to an outsider, he appeared to be a simple farmer, but in actuality, this man was highly respected throughout the mountain villages. He was often consulted for his opinion on political matters, and valued for having had the rare privilege of a fourth grade education. Saadullah was one of only two people that Basnoor was aware of that had the ability to both read and write.

Basnoor handed the telegram to him and asked if he would kindly read the contents of it out loud to her. Saadullah was accustomed to requests such as this, and he was more than happy to oblige this young mother.

Gafoor's message assured Basnoor that he was indeed alive and well; and he spared her unnecessary concern by not disclosing a word about his own struggles. He told her that he had sent money for her by wire, and that she could find it in the care of his trusted friend that lived in the distant village of Hawagali, in the Agror Valley, on the other side of the Indus River.

Basnoor thanked Saadullah, and then she and her sons retraced their steps and returned to their home. She made the necessary arrangements for the children to stay with their grandparents, so that she, accompanied by one of her husband's brothers, could make the long journey to his friend's home.

This would be the first time Basnoor had ever ventured far from Charuna, and while few words were spoken between them, she was grateful for her brother-in-law's guidance, company and protection.

Less than an hour's walk later, they arrived at the river crossing. Gafoor's brother paid the boat attendant a total of four anna to ferry him and Basnoor safely to the other side.   They climbed into the precarious looking, yet solid wooden, flat-bottomed craft, sat down side-by-side on the middle bench and held on.   Fifteen minutes later they reached the other side of the Indus River.

By the end of the first evening, as they were passing through a village, Basnoor and her brother-in-law were invited to stay as honoured guests, and offered lodging and meals. After having traveled mostly on foot for the entire day, they gratefully accepted and settled in for the night.

They were on their way again early the next morning, and reached the friend's house at nightfall. At first light the following day, Basnoor secured the heavy British coins Gafoor had sent - the equivalent of 1,000 rupees - tightly into the folds of her dress for safekeeping during their journey back to Charuna.

It did not take long for news to travel throughout the mountain villages, that Gafoor was not only alive and well, but also prospering in Canada. While Basnoor did not breathe a word of her newfound wealth to anyone, she didn't need to. Once the tailor was summoned to outfit her and the children with new clothes, and she took them to the cobbler to fit them for shoes, it was evidence enough to support the rumours that her financial worries had come to an end. Those that had previously spoken against Gafoor during his inexplicable absence were now singing his praises while making attempts to ingratiate themselves with Basnoor and his parents.

Basnoor would receive telegrams and money transfers from Gafoor with regularity from that point forward.   Gradually, she leased more and more land. While she could always count on assistance from her fellow villagers, this necessitated her to hire a young, impoverished couple that lived nearby, to work the fields. This couple was grateful for the opportunity. They were loyal and worked hard, and they would remain under Basnoor's employ for many years to come.

At long last Basnoor was in a position to save, in the hopes that someday she and her husband could finally build a house of their own.

Their sons enjoyed a typical childhood, and they were each developing their own unique personalities. The eldest boy was wise beyond his years, was most serious and cautious, and the most nurturing of all three. He seemed to have taken on the leading role as the man of the house, and Basnoor counted on him, always confident knowing that he could be trusted to watch out and care for his younger siblings.

The middle child was a playful lad, slightly reckless, and he took delight in making the others laugh. The youngest son was caught in between, and he imitated both of his brothers. He could act as serious as his eldest brother, and in the next moment, play fight with the other.

All three boys were old enough to help their mother and grandparents with the harvesting of the wheat and corn crops, and the milking of the water buffalo.

Although it pained Gafoor to be away from his family, it brought him great satisfaction to know that his earnings, while not without sacrifice, allowed his wife and children to live a decent lifestyle. As time went on, and in order to send as much money as possible home, he would be diligent in keeping his own living expenses low. Once he was satisfied that Basnoor and the children were financially doing well, he began to send money to each of his three brothers, in turn. Gafoor's continued generosity enabled them to comfortably provide for their own wives and children. Consequently, Gafoor would have few luxuries of his own, and continued to live in the cramped quarters of the East Indian bunkhouse for a total of nine long years.

With the assistance of his friends, Gafoor was learning how to read and write, in part so that he could pen his own messages back to India. He tried his best to describe to Basnoor the people he'd met, what he did for a living, and what the land looked like. Gafoor had fallen in love with this new country, and he knew his written attempts fell short when he would try to describe the beauty he'd seen and the liberties he'd experienced. The closest he would ever come to finding the right words happened when he wrote to Basnoor, saying that in Canada, he had truly found heaven on earth.

In 1944 Gafoor received a telegram stating that his father, Ambershah, at the age of 64 had passed away after having fallen ill with fever. Gafoor's foreman, sympathetic to his devastating loss, relieved him from his duties for the rest of his shift. Gafoor would later confess that this turned out to be the saddest day of his life, though he took small consolation upon learning that just before his father died, he had summoned his wife, caressed her hair, and told her, "Come and hug me, I'm leaving now."

Gafoor would continue to work alongside Sir Robert Holland to realize his aspiration of becoming a landed immigrant, and eventually a full citizen in Canada. If he could achieve that, he would then find a way to sponsor each of his family members so that they could join him in Canada. He had learned that this would not be a quick process, but with Sir Robert Holland's knowledge, connections, and assistance, he felt sure to succeed. Gafoor was hopeful, yet naïve, and he had no idea that his struggles with the Department of Immigration were far from over.

7

RAWALPINDI

Gandhi steadfastly maintained his faith that the Muslims, Hindus and Sikhs would eventually iron out and overcome their differences and live together in harmony. Although Gandhi's following continued to grow and he remained true to his beliefs, he would fail to influence the outcome of the final vote to his favour. Following the release of India from British Rule at midnight on August 14, 1947, Pakistan and India would separate. And the partition would not resolve the centuries-old issue of hatred and division between the religions.

Jinnah was appointed and sworn in by the Chief Justice of the Lahore High Court as the first governor-general of Pakistan.[34]

He is quoted as to having said, "... Minorities, to whichever community they may belong will be safeguarded. Their religion or faith or belief will be secure. There will be no interference of any kind with their freedom of worship.   They will have their protection with regard to their religion, faith, their life, their culture. They will be, in all respects, the citizens of Pakistan without any distinction of caste or creed..."[35]

———

Mob attacks, riots, slaughter and retaliation amongst religious factions had become far too commonplace. To name only a few horrific instances, and prior to the separation of Pakistan from India, the Calcutta and Noakhali riots and the Bihar massacre led to the untimely, brutal deaths of approximately 40,000 people. Unfortunately, Rawalpindi would not be immune to atrocities such as these.

The newly independent countries of India and Pakistan each demanded and fought for the accession of Kashmir, which had the misfortune of being situated between the feuding dominions.   October of 1947 would mark the beginning of the first Indo-Pakistani War, or the Kashmir War, and it would result in more than 3,000 known deaths before its end in December of 1948.[36]

———

The railway system in Pakistan (first introduced by British rule in 1855)[37] would experience a major overhaul, including improvements and expansion in 1947, and coincidentally, the very sawmill where Gafoor was employed would produce railway ties to send to his native land.

———

Gafoor reconsidered his tactic, and decided to send money transfers to the care of Basnoor's cousin, rather than to his friend that lived on the other side of the Indus River. Gafoor felt that because this man held a government position in Rawalpindi, the secure arrival of the transfers would be assured, and he knew that he was in proximity to the bank to withdraw the funds on Basnoor's behalf.

It came as no surprise to Basnoor when in early August of 1947, she received another message from her husband stating that money awaited her - however, this time Gafoor asked for something in return. He missed his family terribly. He had not seen the two eldest children for many years, and he had never laid eyes on the youngest child. His request was that she prepare them to travel with her to Rawalpindi, for he'd made arrangements to have their picture taken at a photography studio. Once developed, the picture would be subsequently sent to him by mail. Basnoor immediately took the proper measures to ensure that the farm and home would be well tended to in their absence.

The children were now the ages of 13, 11, and 9, and this would be the first time they'd leave their village. They were excited about going, even though they knew they would only be away for a few days. Basnoor had her reservations about disrupting their ordinary routines and removing them from their familiar environment, but she kept quiet about these concerns. Unfortunately her brother-in-law was away, and she also had misgivings about him not being available to guide and protect her and the children. She packed up their newly made clothes, and she and the children hugged their grandmother goodbye as they began the long journey down the mountain.

With the eldest boy, Nasreen, in the lead, the family of four walked twelve miles down the mountain to the Indus River, paid the attendant, and was ferried across. Once on the other side, they walked a short distance to the village of Darband. Basnoor and the children located the transit station, then patiently stood in line for the bus to take them to Rawalpindi. Once there, they transferred to another bus, which would eventually bring them to Haripur. They were at last nearing the final leg of their journey. Basnoor and the children, after having received directions from the bus driver to find the railway station, climbed aboard a train for the very first time. After an extremely long day and having experienced various modes of transportation, they reached their destination close to midnight.

Similar to 27 years prior, when Gafoor had first reached Rawalpindi, his family arrived, dishevelled, exhausted, dirty and hungry.

Basnoor was anxious as she looked up and down the unfamiliar street. It was dark, streetlights were few and far between, and aside from those at the railway station, the city was nearly void of people. The children were so tired, that they had each sat down cross-legged on the sidewalk.

At last she spotted what she'd been hoping to find. A tonga was headed in their direction, and she waved frantically, hailing it down. The driver steered the horses toward her and pulled up to the curb. She and the children climbed into the carriage, provided the driver with her cousin's address, paid for the ride, and soon after arrived at his house.

Two days later, after they'd rested, Basnoor had the children bathe, and she neatly combed their hair. They changed into their tailored clothing, slipped into their new shoes, and then followed their mother and cousin outdoors to wait for the tonga.

Rawalpindi had changed very little in the years that had passed since Gafoor had first reached it. Motorcars still competed with oxen-pulled carts on the main streets, while the sidewalks were heavily lined with foot traffic. The children were wide-eyed and fascinated, as their carriage passed by wondrous storefronts and made their way through the crowds of oddly dressed people, the likes of which they'd never before seen nor imagined.

It seemed to be a serious matter at Gul Photography, as the boys were directed to sit together in a little room behind the front desk. The middle child most of all, did not understand the concept of remaining motionless for the picture, and he fidgeted, wiggled and moved around until his mother's cousin finally held his head still. The picture was taken, and they promptly returned to his home. It was still well before noon, and their intention was to spend that day and the next resting before beginning their very long trip back to the village.

Another family from Charuna had also arrived to stay with Basnoor's cousin, and while she and the others visited with one another inside the house, her middle child, Jamal went outside to play with his neighbourhood friend, Abdul Aziz. Basnoor knew that Abdul, at fifteen years of age, was a responsible young man, and she felt confident that Jamal would be safe in his care.

After having explored the entire block nearest the house, the boys became restless. Abdul suggested to Jamal, that they go for a walk to visit a mutual relative, Abdul Khanan, who lived near the railway station. Khanan was an uncle to Abdul Aziz, and a brother of Jamal's grandfather - both boys knew him well. Jamal didn't see any harm in the excursion, and he readily agreed to join him.

It could not have possibly occurred to either one of them that in a relatively short period of time, they would inadvertently find themselves stranded in the middle of a battle zone.

The first sound of gunshots rang out less than twenty minutes after they'd left, and to an eleven year old boy, each explosion sounded like a continuous clap of thunder. Jamal stood frozen with fear, as he watched people on the sidewalks, equally caught unaware, scatter madly away from the noise, in the hopes of finding shelter.

A panic stricken man ran straight into the boys, dug his fingers into Abdul's shoulder, and shouted at them before taking off as fast as he could. Unfortunately, the man spoke Urdu, and the boys could not understand what he was saying. They only knew the Pashto language. The reality of their situation finally sunk in, and Abdul reached for Jamal, held him by the arm, then pulled. The boys made brief eye contact, and then they too, broke into a run. They had no choice but to continue moving forward, away and out of the chaos, the line of fire, and farther from the safety of Basnoor's cousin's home.

These two young boys from the remote village of Charuna had suddenly found themselves completely out of their element. Where they'd come from, guns were used for hunting or fired ceremoniously, and they were certainly never used for violent purposes. Neither boy had ever seen the likes of this - there was pandemonium and blood everywhere, as bodies fell in the streets beside them, in front of them, and behind them. They kept their heads low as they scrambled forward - always moving, ducking in and out of alleys, and hoping to find a safe haven in the vicinity of the railway station.

Basnoor had become frantic when, at the first blast of gunfire, she and the other adults hurried outside to bring the boys into the safety of her cousin's home. Sadly, they could find no trace of Jamal or Abdul. With a heavy heart, she returned to the house, and tightly held her youngest and eldest children to her chest.

The boys finally reached the railway station late in the afternoon, and upon immediately being recognized at the home of Abdul Khanan, were quickly steered through the front door. The older man knelt down, tapped each boy on the side of their heads, and in hushed tones, admonished them in Pashto. "What are you doing here? There is a war going on!" The haggard looking, frightened boys were still in shock, and had nothing to say in response.

The fighting raged on relentlessly, and once the first bullet penetrated the house, narrowly missing its inhabitants, it was evidence enough that four walls would no longer ensure anyone's protection. Hunkered low to the ground, Jamal and Abdul stepped lightly as they followed Abdul Khanan and his wife out the back door. Once outside, the four of them climbed the old water pipe that was attached to the side of the house, which led to the roof. The older man reasoned to the others, that should they be discovered hiding there, they at least had the option of jumping to neighbouring rooftops whereas, if they were found inside the house, they would have nowhere to run or hide.

They proceeded to lie flat on their bellies to avoid detection from the crazed gunmen. The noise was constant, as bullets cut through the air, militants shouted and civilians screamed.

For eleven days, Jamal and Abdul remained quiet and still on the rooftop with Abdul Khanan and his wife. Though Jamal was too young to fully understand the depth of everything that was going on around him, he knew enough to mimic the others, making as little noise as possible, while just a short distance below, people were being slaughtered in the streets. Now and then and one by one, each of the four family members would sneak to the edge of the roof, climb down the water pipe, and cup their hands underneath it for a desperately needed drink, or to relieve themselves in the outhouse.

Abdul Khanan's wife was the bravest of them all. They had to eat, and so once each day she would sneak down the water pipe, and into the back door of the house, through to the kitchen to cook a little food to bring back up to the family that lay motionless on the rooftop.

Days passed slowly, each one feeling like a week long, and it seemed as though the carnage surrounding that little house next to the railway station would never end.

Basnoor, two of her sons, and the rest of the family and guests remained huddled quietly in her cousin's house. The adults were exasperated and sick with worry, not knowing the whereabouts nor the fates of either Jamal or Abdul. With the battle endlessly raging outside, it would benefit no one for any of them to consider leaving the house to search for the missing boys.

As a last ditch effort to locate Jamal and Abdul, Basnoor's cousin sent a message to Gafoor's younger brother, who was employed as a railway policeman, ordinarily stationed in the nearby city of Jhelum. If the boys were alive - the only possible place he could think of where they may have sought refuge was at the home of Abdul Khanan and in his message, he begged him to search for them there.

Word of the bloodbath taking place in Rawalpindi had reached all of the remote villages. Every available and able-bodied man - young and old - from each of the Pakhtun tribal regions assembled at the Khyber Pass. Meetings were held in fast order, and it was determined that there was only one way to put an end to the bloodshed. Guns, bullets, knives and spears were collected, before hundreds upon hundreds of these men traveled to the nearest railway station and boarded the trains destined for Rawalpindi.

Early in the morning of the eleventh day, from their hiding place on the rooftop, Jamal, Abdul, Abdul Khanan and his wife, heard the train whistles blow and watched in silence and horror as three heavily loaded trains pulled in to the railway station. It was a sight Jamal would never forget - heavily armed Pakhtun tribesmen, perched on top of the trains, hung off the sides, the fronts, the backs, and crowded the interiors. These men were on a mission as they wildly jumped off before the trains had even come to a full stop.

Within mere hours and true to their word, the men from the tribal regions had put an end to the fighting in Rawalpindi.

The shouting and screaming died down and the firing ceased. Still, the four people on the rooftop dared not move.

Jamal cringed in fear when he thought he heard the sound of his name being called from the alley below. The young boy became more frightened than ever; for he was certain that the fighters had arrived for the sole purpose of getting him.

Jamal heard his name again, and at the urging of Abdul Khanan, crept toward the back of the house. He peeked over the edge and saw a uniformed man, wearing a badge on his shirt, and a gun holstered to his hip, anxiously looking this way and that as he paced alongside the house. As soon as the man looked up, Jamal was in total disbelief as he saw the man's face and realized that this was his uncle. The man spotted Jamal, immediately held his arms open wide and motioned for him to jump.

Gafoor's younger brother led his nephew out of the alley. They had to step over and around bodies that lay haphazardly sprawled in the street in order to reach the railway station. Jamal tried not to look down at them, and focused on the task at hand. At the station, Jamal's uncle was given a green pass that would allow him to travel freely with the boy. He was instructed to tuck it into his belt in such a way that it would remain visible at all times, in the hopes that it would prevent him from being shot at.

It was late in the day by the time Jamal and his uncle arrived at the home of Basnoor's cousin.

Basnoor had almost lost hope that she'd ever see her son again, and cried tears of relief and happiness when at long last, Jamal and his uncle walked into the house.

They would later learn that Jamal's friend, Abdul Aziz, had headed back to Charuna of his own accord that same day.

The fighting had stopped in Rawalpindi, and had moved on in the direction of Kashmir. The people of Rawalpindi were treating their wounded and would soon begin recovering and rebuilding.

It would take another ten days before Basnoor and her cousin felt it safe enough for her to venture outdoors with the children to make their way home. They boarded the train at the station in Rawalpindi and traveled north a great distance, to Haripur. Once there, a bus took them to Darband. By the time they reached Darband it was late in the evening, and much too dark to travel any further. Basnoor rented a little room in a hotel for her and the children to spend the night.

They were served tea bright and early the next morning, before they continued toward home. They walked to the crossing at the Indus River, and the attendant was paid 10 anna to ferry them safely across.

Basnoor and the children climbed into the boat, sat down together on a bench in the middle of it, and fifteen minutes later arrived on their side of the Indus River. With Nasreen again in the lead, they walked for twelve miles up the mountain, before they would reach the security of their beloved and peaceful mountain home.

8

DEPORTATION

In 1948 the United Nations made huge strides towards global cooperation, with the creation of the World Health Organization, and by the adoption of the Universal Declaration on Human Rights. From the time of its inception to present day, this declaration has been translated into nearly 500 languages.[38]

———

On January 30, the sixth attempt to assassinate Gandhi was successful. He took three shots to the chest as he stood near the entrance to the Birla House and soon after he was taken indoors, succumbed to his injuries. The Birla House is now known as Gandhi Smriti, and has been transformed into a museum dedicated to the memory of Gandhi.[39]

———

On September 11, after having been diagnosed with tuberculosis, Jinnah passed away at 71 years old. He lived to see the creation of Pakistan, and he is most well remembered for this legacy that he left behind. December 25th, the day of his birth, is celebrated as a national holiday.

Fatima Jinnah, his youngest sibling, confidante and strongest supporter, continued her campaign in support of the civil rights movement after the death of her beloved brother. Due to her ongoing efforts, she is widely known as Pakistan's *Mother of the Nation*.

———

London hosted the Summer Olympics - the first Games played since they had taken place in Berlin, Germany in 1936. Ordinarily scheduled at four-year intervals, the interruption of the Olympic Games was fully attributed to the seemingly never-ending, far-reaching, Second World War.

———

Sir Robert Holland put forth extra care and special attention toward Gafoor's case - for no monetary gain - and it seemed that this matter had become his personal priority. He had been in constant correspondence with numerous immigration officers and government officials since he'd first met Gafoor in 1940.

Despite his efforts, a disheartening letter addressed to Gafoor arrived in early April of 1948, to the care of his employer in Youbou. It was dated March 30, 1948, and signed by Mr. Taylor, the District Superintendent of the Immigration Branch. Upon receipt of the letter, Gafoor's superintendent promptly called him into his office, asked him to sit down, and then did his best to remain calm as he read the correspondence out loud:

"Dear Sir:

In connection with your application to remain in Canada, I would inform you that after carefully reviewing your case, in view of the fact that you are not admissible to Canada under existing Immigration Regulations, no action can be taken in this matter and it will be necessary for you to effect voluntary departure from Canada within sixty days, failing which it will be necessary for this Department to effect your deportation. Kindly acknowledge receipt of this communication."[40]

Needless to say, this was not the response that Gafoor had been hoping or expecting to receive, and he was devastated. With his superintendent's help, Gafoor appealed in writing to Mr. Taylor and received in short order, a further response to the care of his employer who, after again insisting that Gafoor sit down, read it out to him:

"Dear Sir:

Answering your letter of the 3rd instant wherein you ask if you can make a further appeal against the Department's decision with regard to your deportation, may I inform you that your appeal has already been dealt with by the Minister of this Department and unless there was some additional evidence produced I do not see where anything can be gained by your further representation.   Yours Truly."[41]

Gafoor swiftly made arrangements to meet with Sir Robert Holland as soon as possible.   Upon reviewing the letters, Sir Robert Holland advised Gafoor that neither of them should give up so easily nor admit defeat. He had recently been in direct communications with Dr. Hugh Keenleyside, a well-known Canadian diplomat, and he decided that the best course of action would be to write to him again. So far, all responses to Gafoor's application for landed immigrant status had been unfavourable.

Gafoor received a letter from Sir Robert Holland dated April 22nd which included a copy of the letter he'd written to Dr. Keenleyside the day before.   As evidenced by that letter, Sir Robert Holland was clearly running out of patience:

"Dear Dr. Keenleyside:

I am greatly obliged for your telegram, in reply to my letter of April 16th regarding the case of John Mohammed (Gafoor Khan).

I enclose a copy of a letter dated April 18th from John Mohammed to Mr. Taylor, District Superintendent of the Immigration Branch in Vancouver, begging for an extension of the time-limit of sixty days expiring May 30th, within which he is ordered to depart from Canada.

Perhaps this could be taken as his appeal against the order, but if a formal appeal from him is required, I will call him from Youbou and arrange for it to be dispatched by air mail.

The facts of his case are no doubt fully stated in your records. As I understand them, they are as follows.

John Mohammed arrived on the B.C. coast as an oiler on the P&O ship "Rajputana" about ten years ago, jumped ship, and became an illegal immigrant, as did a good many other illegal immigrant East Indians at that time. He found work in the logging industry and has been an employee of the B.C. Forest Products Company Ltd. and its predecessor, Industrial Timber Mills Ltd., for the last eight years. I enclose a copy of a certificate given to him by the Mill Superintendent, Mr. Whittaker, and also enclose a letter written to me by Mr. Jeyes, the Chief Accountant of the Company, Cowichan Division. These are strong testimony, in my opinion, to his worthiness and to his ability as an employee.

Dr. D.P. Pandia, an eminent Indian from the Madras Province, who has been in Canada for some time effectively advocating the cause of East Indians in B.C. (and who is now at the Chateau Laurier in Ottawa), suggested to John Mohammed that he should endeavor to regularize his position by applying to the Canadian Government for permission to remain in the country. Dr. Pandia has, I believe, successfully pleaded the cause of other East Indian "illegal immigrants" and obtained for them the necessary papers.

But unfortunately John Mohammed's application was not successful, and it seems possible that, if he had remained in obscurity and not brought his case to notice, nobody would have troubled to dig it up and he could have continued to live his humble and useful life at Youbou. If I am right in this, it may perhaps be regarded as a point in his favor that he voluntarily revealed himself and submitted his petition.

His appeal against the deportation order must rest simply on the fact that, though he entered Canada illegally ten years ago, he had made good and proved himself to be the kind of man that would wreck his life, because he has become thoroughly Canadianized, has forgotten Hindustani, though he remembers his local language, Pashtu, spoken in the Hazara district from where he came; and if he went back, he would find it extremely hard to earn a living as a cultivator. He has worked and saved and supported his wife and three children in India in the hope that at some day it might be possible for him to get them over to Canada, but even if that is not possible, he wants to be allowed to remain here because he knows that by doing so he can support them in comfort.

The one point which might be considered as prejudicing his claim to remain in Canada is that he is not literate in English. He has a colloquial knowledge of English which serves his need, but he has never been taught and he comes from a thick-headed but honest and faithful peasantry with little aptitude for book-learning. I was in India for thirty

years and I can vouch that he comes from good
stock and is an honest and worthy man.

I am deeply interested in his case because I know
what a tragedy it will be for him if he is forced to
leave Canada.

I would gladly vouch for him that he would not
disappear into the blue, if the deportation order is
stayed pending consideration of his case. What is
worrying him at the moment is the fear that he may
be seized by the police and held on May 30th in
custody pending deportation. If he could be
reassured on this point, it would be a great relief to
his mind, and he would be able to go on working
cheerfully pending the final decision, at all events.

I believe that, if his deportation had to be
effected, the C.P.R. have no ships now running to the
Orient, nor are they likely to have any for a long time
to come. If I am right in this, it would not be a
practical possibility to deport John Mohammed for a
long while to come, and so it would seem to be the
best course to let him continue working where he is
for the time being, under guarantee, if required, that
he will not try to hide himself.

I have written to Sir Zafrulla Khan, who is, I
believe, High Commissioner Designate for Pakistan
in Canada, to try to interest him in the case, as John
Mohammed's home village is in the Hazara District
of Pakistan, and he is of course a Moslem.

I hope very much that the Government may find

it possible to stretch the letter of the law a little in John Mohammed's case and include him in the number of "illegal immigrants" whose position as residents of Canada has, I believe already been regularized.

I will gladly furnish any other information about John Mohammed that may be required.

With kind regards."[42]

Sir Robert Holland was not about to let this rest. He continued to write letters and make telephone calls to government agencies and officials; leaving no stone unturned, his letter appealing to Sir Zafrulla Khan, who was in fact, the Foreign Minister of Pakistan, presented Gafoor's case in full detail.

At last, Sir Robert Holland received a letter dated May 18, 1948, from an Immigration Branch superintendent that seemed promising. To personally reassure Gafoor, he scribbled at the top of the letter, "*All is well, REH*" and forwarded it directly to Gafoor's attention at the Youbou sawmill.

"Dear Sir Robert:

Referring to our telephone conversation yesterday in the case of Gafoor Khan or John Mohammed, I would advise that at the time I did not have this man's file before me and was not as familiar with his case as Mr. Taylor, however after your call I found that when speaking to you I had another man in mind but find that the case of Gafoor Khan is now before the Department and that there is every indication that he is being favourably dealt with. However when I am advised in the matter by the Department I shall again write you of the decision rendered. In the meantime Gafoor Khan has returned to his work on the Island and will await advice from us."[43]

While Gafoor kept to his routine, putting in the usual ten-hour days, six days a week on the green chain, Sir Robert Holland continued working faithfully in the background on his behalf. At the very least, they each felt assured knowing that Gafoor would be permitted to continue to work while awaiting the final decision made by the Department of Immigration.

Gafoor had now been in Canada for the better part of nine years, and at times he worried that he'd never be granted legal status. He felt as though he was living on borrowed time, and worried constantly that he could be detained at any moment. The ongoing support and encouragement of his friends, co-workers and the superintendent were effective in helping to keep his spirits high.

On June 9, 1948 Dr. Keenleyside wrote his reply to Sir Robert Holland, to advise him that steps were being taken to grant Gafoor legal standing in Canada.

"Dear Sir Robert:

In continuation of my letter dated May 4th, 1948, I am pleased to advise action has now been taken to provide for Gafoor Khan's legal admission to this country by Order-In-Council. The Pacific District Superintendent of Immigration is, therefore, being advised to take the necessary action to grant Gafoor

Khan a legal landing in Canada."[44]

Shortly thereafter, yet another telegram was received at the Youbou sawmill, and Gafoor was summoned to the office. Gafoor immediately thought that his days at the sawmill were officially finished, for he felt certain that his superintendent held his deportation order in his hand. This time, the superintendent waved the paper around in the air, and for once, did not ask Gafoor to sit down. Instead, he reached for Gafoor's hand, shook it and smiled. "Congratulations, Gafoor. You are now a landed Canadian citizen. Take the rest of the day off with pay, and celebrate your freedom."

Gafoor couldn't believe his ears. After running and stressing for so long - these worries had come to an end. Gafoor walked straight to the East Indian bunkhouse, sat down on a log behind it, and wept tears of joy.

At his soonest opportunity, he prepared a message to Basnoor, that stated, "I am now a landed Canadian citizen." The biggest battle of his life was finally over.

Gafoor's message was sent by telegram, courtesy of Sir Robert Holland to Gafoor's close friend, Nawab Sir Muhammad Farid Khan, who ruled the princely state of Amb[45] on the other side of the Indus River. The Nawab immediately summoned a messenger, and before dispatching him to the village of Charuna, instructed him to personally hand deliver and read out loud, the telegram bearing the good news to Gafoor's wife.

Basnoor's dream had also come true - she had finally saved enough of the money that Gafoor had sent, to build a house for her family. She hired the workers needed to cut and plane lumber to make and raise the roof, and for each of the supporting beams. Men from all of the nearby villages came together and volunteered their time and energy, lifting stones and painting clay until it was finished. By the time 1948 neared its end, Basnoor and the three children were at long last, able to move out of Gafoor's parents' home.

9

NASREEN

The Canadian Pacific Railway ("CPR") incorporated in 1881, and best known for providing rail services linking the east to the west, was highly instrumental in the development of the prairie provinces, and this was accomplished by selling off parcels of land, often ready-made farms, to encourage the migration of settlers and immigrants.[46]

As early as 1884, the CPR expanded its horizons and entered into the business of shipping. British Columbia Coast Steamships (BCCSS)[47] was formed, and the coastal vessels offered sailings between Vancouver Island and the mainland, and (including, but not limited to) Seattle, Washington, and as far away as Alaska.

———

Liaquat Ali Khan,[48] referred to by Jinnah as his right hand man, had more than proven his political prowess and after previously having served as finance minister[49], was appointed the first prime minister of Pakistan on August 15, 1947.[50] During his early years, he attended Oxford and earned his law degree, and later had worked diligently alongside Jinnah for the independence of Pakistan. His aspirations seemed to know no bounds - he was a member of the Muslim League, and he had held numerous high-ranking government positions, including having served for a brief period of time as the Foreign Minister of Pakistan.

In 1950, Liaquat Ali Khan met with the prime minister of India, and after days of discussion, they each agreed to and signed the Liaquat-Nehru Pact.[51]

This pact or treaty was intended to clearly set down and ensure the rights of Indian and Pakistani minorities. Tensions and riots between the two countries had only increased since the partition and both sides wished to avoid yet another full scale war. The pact was effective, and resulted in stiff consequences for those that broke the laws decreed and enforced by the pact.

———

In 1950, the Korean War began when South Korea was invaded by North Korea. This war would last for more than three years and by its end, two and a half million lives would be lost.

———

By law, Gafoor would be required to maintain his status as a landed immigrant for four years, before becoming eligible to qualify for full Canadian citizenship. However, as a landed immigrant, he had most rights that a full citizen would; the only exceptions being that he was not entitled to vote in elections, nor could he obtain a Canadian passport. These limitations were of no consequence to him or to his needs at that time.

His new status allowed him the liberty to begin the process of sponsoring his family members. With the help of his friend, Sir Robert Holland, Gafoor submitted his first application to sponsor his eldest son, fifteen-year-old Nasreen. One year would pass before this application would succeed.

Finally in a position to plan for his future, and in anticipation of his family's arrival, Gafoor knew that the time had come for him to build a house. The nearby, recently incorporated town of Lake Cowichan was larger than Youbou, and offered most amenities, including a school, a grocery store, a post office, a bank, and an RCMP station. Inevitably, Gafoor saw this community as having the potential of becoming his family's ideal future home. He paid a visit to the bank, where he applied and qualified for a loan that enabled him to purchase two adjoining lots on Poplar Street.

Gafoor had begun to lay the groundwork to ensure that he would no longer have to live out of his suitcase. Most importantly to Gafoor, was the comfort he took in knowing that his son would not have to stay in the bunkhouse once he arrived.

As soon as he had title to the properties, Gafoor moved out of the East Indian bunkhouse and into a small shed that sat on one of his newly acquired lots - this shed was to become his very last temporary living quarters.

Gafoor enlisted the help and guidance of his eager friends and co-workers that were skilled in house building. In the evenings, after their shifts ended at the sawmill, they gathered for days on end, graph paper, pencils, erasers and rulers in hand, and worked together until the house design was decided on and the final blueprints were sketched.

They would build a one and a half storey, three bedroom, two bathroom house. The main floor would hold the kitchen, full bathroom, living room and two bedrooms and it would suit him, Basnoor, and the two younger boys. The second floor would become a suite, in anticipation of his eldest son's future needs, and would consist of one bedroom, a half bathroom and a smaller kitchen. The supply list and costs were then roughly calculated and before long, they were ready to begin.

With pride, Gafoor deftly handled the sledgehammer as he drove the first stakes into the ground. He helped snap the chalk line, and all the while learning, watched with excitement as the basement was excavated and the footings were dug. Gafoor worked alongside his friends, with the framing and the placing of the rebar before the concrete was poured. This would be a long, drawn out process. Gafoor's loan only covered the cost of the land, and the actual building supplies would be purchased as he could afford to pay for them.

The first order of lumber was delivered, each board perfectly planed and stacked in order of use and size. Gafoor would often reflect how greatly this house differed from the home of his youth; put together by a handful of men using screws, nails and wood, rather than his days of old, when dozens of villagers would labour from dawn until dusk, to painstakingly create homes built of heavy stone and clay.

In order to apply for his passport, Nasreen would have to travel for days at a time to reach the nearest passport office that was located in Abbottabad[52]. Accompanied by one of his uncles, they made multiple trips that entailed walking down the mountain to reach Rawalpindi, crossing the Indus River, and catching both bus and train to reach Abbottabad. For reasons unknown, the processing of his application was repeatedly delayed. Exasperated, they took the train to the head office in Peshawar to inquire, but were advised to make their inquiries in Abbottabad. After nearly a year of unsuccessful round-trips and attempts at the passport office, Nasreen eventually succeeded and returned to the village, passport in hand. A message was sent by telegram to Gafoor, who by this time had Nasreen's sponsorship in place, and with Sir Robert Holland's assistance, immediately arranged his flight.

Nasreen's plane left Karachi[53] and stopped at the airport in Ellis Island, New York, where he was scheduled to transfer to another plane that was bound for Vancouver.

Mass confusion ensued as Nasreen tried to pass through customs. He was held in custody for not holding in his possession, a United States visa. Speaking and understanding only Pashto, the young boy was unable to explain his reason for landing in New York, and could not speak in his own defense.

Sir Robert Holland made immediate inquiries at the United States Customs Department, and on July 3rd, 1950 received this reply on Gafoor's behalf:

"Dear Sir:

With reference to your telegram to the Embassy of Pakistan, Washington, D.C. regarding your son M. Nasreen Khan, which was forwarded on to this office, enquiries were made of the United States Immigration and Naturalization Services at Ellis Island, New York, and today we dispatched the following telegram to you:

"US IMMIGRATION ADVISE NASREEN KHAN LEFT NEW YORK SUNDAY EVENING 2nd JULY FOR BRITISH COLUMBIA CANADA"

Your son was apparently held for verification of departure from New York as he did not possess a visa for the United States.

I trust that by the time you receive this letter, you will have been reunited with your son."[54]

Slightly worse for wear, Nasreen finally arrived in Canada and was indeed, reunited with his father. Gafoor picked him up from the airport in Vancouver, and they rode a British Columbia Coast Steamship across the Pacific Ocean to the port in Nanaimo. From there, they took the bus to Lake Cowichan. Once his son had a chance to settle in, Gafoor showed him around the town, and then brought him to the Youbou sawmill. Fortunately, the mill was in the process of hiring new workers. Nasreen was immediately hired, trained, and began working on the green chain alongside Gafoor.

10

ASSASSINATION

In 1951, King George VI and his wife, Queen Elizabeth had scheduled a trip for Canada, but he had become seriously ill. His eldest daughter, Princess Elizabeth II, accompanied by her husband, Phillip, the Duke of Edinburgh, went in their place. This would be their first visit to Canada, and their 16,000-kilometer tour included travel by air, train and sea.

Upon her return to the United Kingdom, she is quoted as to having said about the country she had just visited, "I am sure that nowhere under the sun could one find a land more full of hope, of happiness and of fine, loyal, generous-hearted people."[55]

———

The Korean War was still going strong, and 16 member countries of the United Nations, fighting to assist South Korea, were involved. Even though armistice talks between the north and south divisions began in 1951, the agreement would not be signed nor come into effect until 1953 and in the meantime the fighting continued.

Before the Korean War's end, more than 26,000 Canadians would serve - of this number, 516 lost their lives[56] and over 1,200 were wounded.

———

Along with the separation of Pakistan from India, came a number of citizenship issues and refugee crises affecting the Muslims who had migrated from India to the new, Muslim majority state of Pakistan. With an eye toward solving the ongoing problems, the government enacted the Pakistan Citizenship Act to outline the provisions of citizenship, in 1951.[57]

———

On October 16th, 1951 while preparing to make an important announcement at a public gathering in Rawalpindi, Liaquat Ali Khan, the first prime minister of Pakistan would be assassinated.[58]

The police, in attendance for ordinary security purposes immediately located then shot and killed the assassin, who was later identified as, Saad Akbar Babrak. Widespread speculation and conspiracy theories are ongoing to this day, as to whether Babrak was a hired killer or an individual fanatic following through with his own agenda.[59]

Later, the park that the prime minister was shot in would be renamed, *Liaquat Bagh* to honour his memory. Posthumously, Liaquat would be known as *Shaheed-e-Millat*, meaning, *Martyr of the Nation*, and his final resting place is in the National Mausoleum in Karachi, alongside his good friend, Muhhamad Ali Jinnah.

———

His wife, Begum Ra'ana Liaquat Ali Khan who had become the First Lady[60] upon his appointment as Prime Minister, had previously acted for the Pakistan Movement Committee under Jinnah. Concerned about an imminent war between British India and Japan, and having recognized her leadership potential, Jinnah had told her, "Be prepared to train the women. Islam doesn't want women to be shut up and never see fresh air."[61]

These words she took to heart, and she had become an advocate and pioneer for the rights of Muslim women and children. Begum Ra'ana Liaquat Ali Khan's political career continued after her husband's death, and throughout her lifetime, she would enjoy multiple political accomplishments. For instance, she formed the Pakistan Women's National Guard in 1949, she was the first United Nations Muslim woman delegate, and she co-founded the Pakistan Women's Association with Fatima Jinnah. On separate occasions, she served as Pakistan's ambassador to the Netherlands, Tunisia and Italy; other honours include having earned the Woman of Achievement Medal, the United Nation's Human Rights Award, and she will forever be known as, *The Mother of Pakistan.*

———

Basnoor's farming income had grown substantially over the years, and this afforded her and her two young sons the luxury of visiting their cousin's home in Rawalpindi with more frequency. She and the boys looked forward to taking time away from their endless chores at home, and each had safely tucked their memories of what had occurred during the Rawalpindi riots just a few years prior, to the back recesses of their minds.

By now, the boys were quite accustomed to the sights, sounds, and smells of the city. They no longer felt wary nor quite as awestruck while in Rawalpindi, and they fervently looked forward to each new trip. They made plans to visit their cousin in October of 1951. At this time, the youngest boy would soon be 13, and Jamal was only a month shy of turning 15 years of age.

Basnoor granted Jamal permission to travel a few blocks down the road to a movie theatre to watch a picture show. A co-worker and close friend of his cousin, Jummah Khan would join him, and he suggested that if they left soon enough, they could watch and hear the Prime Minister speak at the Muslim City League meeting, which was being held at a park near the movie theatre. Jamal eagerly agreed, for he had only previously listened to the Prime Minister's speeches above the static, through his battery-operated radio. He looked forward to this rare opportunity to see him in person.

It was early in the day, when the two young men promptly stepped into their shoes, threw on their sweaters, and left the house to stand on the street and await the next available tonga. Luck was on their side -

their wait was not long, and Jamal and Jummah were soon on their way down Muree Road. The tonga driver courteously dropped them off as near as he could to the park.

Municipal Park, also known as Company Bagh, covered a large area of land and, centrally located, it was easily accessible from most parts of the city. It was famous for its beauty, and well known as a key location for hosting public political gatherings. On this day in particular, the Prime Minister was scheduled to make an important announcement. Jamal and Jummah were excited as they entered the park from Murree Road, where they joined thousands of other like-minded civilians. Together, they slipped through the crowds to stand closer to the stage, confident that they would have a clear view of the Prime Minister without any difficulty from where they stood.

This would be a great day - Jamal checked his wristwatch and confirmed that they'd still have plenty of time to see the show once the speech was finished.

Two serious looking dignitaries dressed in suits walked across the stage and affixed a megaphone to the podium, which stood tall in the center, toward the front. The electrical cord was unwound and rolled under the back curtain and its plug was inserted into a concealed outlet. Their tasks complete, the two men quietly stepped back, arms folded across their chests, and waited. All eyes were upon them, and the steady murmur among the audience began to quiet in anticipation of the Prime Minister's arrival.

Jamal couldn't help but feel grateful that he would soon be in the presence of greatness. From a young age, he'd been made aware of the significant role Liaquat Ali Khan had played, not only in the independence of India from British Rule, but also in the creation of Pakistan as an independent state.

At last, the Prime Minister took to the stage, and the audience waved, clapped and cheered as he neared the podium. All became quiet again when Liaquat Ali Khan picked up the megaphone and depressed the trigger. The air filled with dramatic crackles and pops; he raised the megaphone to his lips and was about to begin.

Two shots rang out in fast succession, and just as quickly, the megaphone hit the floor, and the Prime Minister - whose chest had turned crimson - crumpled and fell backwards on the stage.

Only for a brief period did time stand still. In the next moment, there was mass hysteria.

More shots rang out before the innocent spectators regained their senses all at once. Dizzy with fear, panic and confusion, people ran in all directions, and screams filled the air. Jamal and Jummah sped toward the movie theatre and had barely made it through the front doors before the gates were slammed shut and locked behind them.

Any thoughts of watching a picture show were now the furthest thing from Jamal's mind. Hours would pass before the doors of the movie theatre were opened and the gates to the grounds eventually unlocked. Darkness had set in by the time Jamal and Jummah - still in disbelief - were able to head back to his cousin's house. As they walked, they could plainly see the lights of a plane as it flew overhead toward Pakistan's capital, the city of Karachi.

The radio was playing loudly when they reached the house, and it was announced that the Prime Minister had survived the assassination attempt.

It would not be until the next morning, when the radio was turned on again, that everyone would learn that the shots were fatal. Prime Minister Liaquat Ali Khan had been rushed by plane to the hospital in Karachi for medical treatment, but he died shortly after arriving there.

11

JAMAL

In February of 1953, the esteemed Pakistan Academy of Sciences was established in Lahore, and its official inauguration attracted over 1,000 esteemed guests from various scientific communities across the globe. The Academy, now located in Islamabad[62], has since grown to include chapters in Karachi, Lahore, Peshawar and Quetta.[63]

———

In June of 1953, Princess Elizabeth II, next in line to the throne, celebrated her coronation and was officially pronounced the Queen of England. History was made, as this event would mark the first televised British coronation.[64]

Her reign as monarch included seven countries: the United Kingdom, Canada, Australia, New Zealand, the Union of South Africa, Pakistan and Ceylon. Among those present at the coronation were the Prime Ministers of India, Pakistan and Canada.

———

Benazir Bhutto, who would become Pakistan's first female prime minister 35 years later, was born in Karachi on June 21, 1953. She would hold office from 1988 until 1990, and then again from 1993 until 1996, making her the first, and to present day, the only prime minister in Pakistan to ever serve twice.[65] She was assassinated at Liaquat Bagh on December 27, 2007 and the following year, was awarded the United Nations Prize in the field of Human Rights.[66]

———

Pakistan is home to two of the top ten highest mountain ranges in the world. K2, so named under British rule, is second in height only to Mount Everest, and belongs to the Karakoram mountain range.[67]

Nanga Parbat, which means, *Naked Mountain* in the Urdu language, is the 9th highest mountain in the world, the second most prominent peak of the Himalayas, and it lies south of the Indus River in Pakistan. Accounts of climbers attempting to ascend this mountain date back as early as the 1800s, and the first successful ascent was made in 1953.[68]

———

In 1954, Pakistan adopted its State Emblem, and the National Anthem, or *Qaumi Taranah* was adopted and officially recognized. The music for this song was initially composed five years prior in 1949, and the lyrics did not follow until 1952.[69]

———

By the time 1953 made its appearance, Gafoor had been away from his family and native country for fourteen years, and had been enjoying his employment in Youbou for nearly as long. He had learned to read English well enough to scan the weekly newspaper and he could pick out the newsworthy items that occasionally caught his interest.

Steady progress was being made in the construction of his house on Poplar Street - it was roofed and framed in its entirety, and the top floor was nearly complete. In the meantime, the shed was comfortable enough to accommodate Gafoor's and Nasreen's basic needs, and they continued to reside in it.

Nasreen was now nearing twenty years of age, and from the time he'd arrived in Canada, he had also maintained steady employment at the sawmill. Gafoor was proud of his son, and although he predicted that Nasreen would have a bright future ahead of him on the green chain, Nasreen had ideas of his own.

Before he'd left Pakistan, he'd met and fallen in love with a respectable young lady - and his heart was set on marrying her. Despite Gafoor's protests, Nasreen returned to Pakistan during the latter part of 1953, to do just that. He would enjoy a tearful yet happy reunion with his mother and brothers once he was settled back in his native land.

Gafoor did not yet have the financial resources to sponsor his wife and two younger sons, but he was confident that he could sponsor one of them. So began the next sponsorship application - he would apply to have his sixteen-year-old son, Jamal join him in Canada.

Gafoor contacted and arranged to meet with his friend, Sir Robert Holland, and with his assistance, again submitted all of the necessary documents to the Department of Immigration.

In his attempts to obtain a passport, Jamal would face delays similar to those that his brother had encountered years before.

Due to Nasreen's detainment at Ellis Island while on his way to Canada, Jamal had learned that in order to apply for his passport and have it stamped accordingly, he would first need to obtain a letter of reference. This would have to be written and signed by a police official, verifying that he was a law-abiding citizen. As soon as time allowed him to leave the village, he and his favourite uncle, Rehmat Shah, made their way to the nearest police station for that purpose.

Jamal and Rehmat explained the reason for their visit, whereupon the police inspector laughed and said, "A doctor cannot remedy himself." He was not willing to swear that Jamal was law-abiding based on the word of Jamal, nor his uncle, and he suggested that they ask a village elder or chief[70] to speak on his behalf instead.

As Jamal and Rehmat were leaving, they overheard the police inspector explaining to the superintendent that Jamal's father, Gafoor, was waiting for him in Canada. The two men were called back to the police station, and waited patiently while the inspector wrote and signed the letter of reference.

Accompanied again by his uncle, Jamal made numerous trips to the passport office in the city of Abbottabad. The clerk was polite and cheerful, but would time and again dismiss him with a wave, and advise that he return at a later date.

Overcome with frustration, Jamal finally asked why his application had not yet been processed. The clerk explained that his application was being delayed at the head office in Peshawar. Jamal and Rehmat took the next available train to Peshawar, where they were kindly told to return to Abbottabad to inquire. At this point, the two disheartened men had no choice but to return to Charuna. Too much time had been wasted and they each had chores that had fallen behind on the farm.

Jamal and Rehmat were on their way back to Rawalpindi, but they would first have to transfer to another bus once they reached Haripur. Much to their delight, they realized that the bus they were to ride in was brand new - they eagerly climbed aboard, to sit next to a distinguished looking gentleman in the front seat. Jamal closed the door hard behind them, just as he would have done if this were an older model transport. Jamal heard a cracking sound, and the glass in the door window had shattered by the time he sheepishly took his seat.

The gentleman they were sitting next to promptly stood up, turned around and introduced himself to the rest of the passengers. He happened to be a well-known and respected politician. Without hesitation he instructed them that no one should tell the bus driver, upon his return, who was responsible for breaking the glass. While Jamal felt horrible for what he'd done, he would be eternally grateful for the man's random act of kindness, for he had in effect ensured Jamal and

Rehmat's safe, uninterrupted passage home.

Despite his inquires, not a word was spoken to the bus driver - once he'd returned - about the broken glass. He was not happy as he closed the doors, started the engine and drove down the road away from Haripur.

In anticipation of his stop, the gentleman stood up and pulled the cord. The bus came to a halt, and Jamal watched in wonder as the gentleman faded into the streets of his very own village - a village that had been gifted to him by the Nawab of Amb.

The crops had to be taken off before Jamal could find an opportunity to leave again. The next time, he planned to enlist the help of his older brother who was now happily married, and working and living in Rawalpindi.

On a similar return trip to Charuna, Jamal was on his way through Haripur when he had begun to feel unwell. He was dizzy as he attempted to shrug it off, and he attributed his fever to a likely contaminated kebab he'd recently purchased from a roadside food stand. He continued walking as best he could, toward the bus station.

By the time he boarded the bus scheduled for Darband, Jamal was sweating profusely and he struggled just to keep his eyes open. He felt his throat swelling, and breathing took all of his effort. He shared a bench seat next to a young boy who was on his way home, and who would be getting off at the next stop. The boy, genuinely concerned about Jamal's welfare, invited him to return with him to his home so he could rest.

After spending two days shivering, coughing and slipping in and out of consciousness, Jamal was determined to return to his mother's care in Charuna. His condition had worsened, but he felt that he should not be taking advantage of the young boy, nor his family's generosity any longer. He thanked his host family for their kindness, and staggered to the bus station. He climbed aboard, suffered through the rough 27 mile bus ride, and was barely conscious by the time he reached Darband.

That very same day, Gafoor was busy working on the green chain as usual, when he was summoned to the office. A telegram had just arrived to his attention from his friend, Saadullah Khan. This was completely unexpected, and Gafoor was puzzled as he opened the envelope. He had no idea that he was about to find that his very worst fear as a parent would soon be realized.

The message stated that Jamal was deathly ill in a hospital in Rawalpindi, and requested that Gafoor send money for medicine.

Gafoor kept reading, and learned that Saadullah had been visiting friends in Darband, when he had, by pure chance, come across Gafoor's son. Jamal, on his way home to Charuna, had stopped to rest at the hotel just as Saadullah was passing by. He recognized Jamal immediately, and he could plainly see that the young man was in dire need of medical attention. Saadulah set his own plans aside and took charge of the situation. He sent a messenger to speak with Basnoor, and stayed with Jamal until she arrived.

While extremely grateful to his friend, Gafoor was beside himself with grief and worry. He silently said a prayer for Jamal's healing, and immediately arranged for the money transfer, along with a telegram, begging that his son not be allowed to die.

Basnoor had dropped everything once the messenger had reached her, and she immediately made haste for Darband. Once she arrived she was devastated, for Basnoor had never before seen anyone that appeared to be so near death. With Saadulah's help, she and Jamal boarded the first bus bound for Rawalpindi.

They arrived at her cousin's house, who arranged for him to see the doctor. While the doctor agreed that Jamal was not well, he was not able to determine the cause of Jamal's illness. From there, Basnoor and her cousin took Jamal to the hospital, where he was properly diagnosed. Somehow during the course of his travels, Jamal had come in contact with, and had contracted the dreaded and often fatal diphtheria virus.

Jamal was hurried to a room, laid on a bed, changed into a gown, and hooked up to receive medicine intravenously. Basnoor was frightened, and she felt helpless as she watched the needle inserted into her son's vein. As the medications were being administered, the exhausted young man slept. He would not open his eyes again for sixteen hours.

Because he had been on the brink of death, feverish, and semi-conscious most of the time, Jamal's memories of his hospital stay would be few. He would recollect times when the nurses had to pick him up from the floor where he'd passed out, and in particular, he would for the rest of his days, remember his roommate.

Jamal would not discover his name nor what ailed him, but he would never forget his face, nor his heartbreaking words.

About a week after Jamal had first been admitted, he began to improve and spent less time asleep, and more time awake. Jamal guessed that his roommate might be roughly five years his senior - also a young man. One day, he looked Jamal straight in the eye, smiled weakly and said, "I'm not going to make it, but I'm glad you are going to get better. Allah be with you."

One week later, Gafoor's prayers were answered when Jamal was released from the hospital.

Upon his return home, it took some time for Jamal to regain his energy and strength. His colour had returned, the chills were gone, and slowly, his appetite was improving.

The doctor had informed both Jamal and Basnoor that it was not possible for all of the symptoms he'd experienced to be diphtheria-related, and it was highly likely that in addition to the virus, he'd had food poisoning from the kebab.

As soon as he was well enough to travel, Jamal and Nasreen rode the bus to Abbottabad to ask about his passport and again, Jamal was told to return another time. Irritated beyond belief, Jamal marched straight passed the clerk's desk, and to the office of the superintendent. After introducing himself, Jamal was well prepared to demand that his passport application be processed. To his great surprise, the superintendent smiled, shook his hand and told him that his passport was ready, and handed it to him.

Soon after the young men had each returned to their homes, a telegram was prepared and sent to Gafoor. The sponsorship papers had already been approved and Gafoor immediately secured the travel arrangements for Jamal.

Jamal bade a tearful farewell to his mother, Basnoor, his youngest brother, his grandmother, and the rest of his friends and relatives. He picked up his suitcase, waved at his loved ones, and took one last look at his home before heading down the forest path that would eventually lead him to Rawalpindi.

Nasreen awaited Jamal's arrival - the two brothers walked to the railway station and boarded the train bound for Karachi. After numerous stops to drop off and pick up more passengers, they arrived in the city over 960 miles later, and twenty-four long hours after they'd first climbed aboard.

The two brothers would stay with a childhood friend from their village. Thankfully, Rasool Khan lived and worked in Karachi, and he insisted that Jamal and Nasreen stay as honoured guests in his humble home. In true Pakhtunwali fashion, he welcomed them heartily, and provided them with meals and lodging.

They stayed with Rasool for ten days while waiting for Jamal's appointment at the Canadian Embassy - he needed to have his passport stamped in order to be permitted access to Canada.

The Canadian Embassy was located in the impressive Metropole Hotel, and it covered much of the third floor.

The Metropole Hotel had officially opened only three years prior, and in a relatively short period of time had become famous as a world-class tourist destination. The hotel held business offices and a nightclub, and it drew celebrities the likes of Ava Gardner, the Shah of Iran and King Hussein.

Jamal followed Nasreen through the large double

doors and he felt as though he had stepped into an entirely different world. Heavily laden, cloth draped banquet tables lined the far wall, and servants walked about, carrying trays full of appetizers. He was certain that there were more people inside the hotel than outdoors, in the entire city of Karachi. The women were adorned with jewels and wore elegant dresses, and all of the men wore suits. Jamal shook his head, wondering if people always dressed and acted this way in Karachi. He looked down at his own clothes - he'd worn his best pants and shirt for the occasion- and while not ashamed, he was aware that his attire paled in comparison.

Nasreen led him through the milling crowd and straight to the staircase that would take them to the Canadian Embassy.

The clerk at the desk was friendly, but she was Canadian, and spoke in English. Nasreen took charge; after having spent three years learning the language in Canada, would translate for his younger brother. The clerk was excited as she went on to explain to Nasreen that the hotel was preparing for an honoured guest's arrival - Sir Sultan Muhammed Shah, better known as Aga Khan III,[71] a prominent politician and wealthy race horse enthusiast, was due to make his presence known at any moment. Nasreen explained this to Jamal, and it was then that he understood the reason for the activity they'd witnessed on the main floor, as well as the motorcade that had previously passed them as they'd walked along the street.

Nasreen was instructed to surrender the passport for review. If it was approved, it would be stamped as requested, and he could pick it up again in ten days' time.

Ten days later, Jamal followed his brother back to the Metropole and retrieved his passport. There were no more obstacles standing in his way, and he was booked for the three o'clock flight to England.

12

HOME

The two brothers rode the bus from the station nearest the Metropole Hotel to the airport. Jamal was delighted to see that everyone from Charuna - that is - those that were living and working in Karachi, awaited their arrival at the airport to see him off. There were so many hugs, prayers and well wishing that he thought his heart might burst with love and gratitude.

Nasreen would be the last person that Jamal would bid farewell to. His strong, older brother - the one always relied on to lead, guide and protect his younger brothers, had tears in his eyes when the time came. Jamal had never before seen him cry. They walked together until Nasreen was not permitted by airport security to continue any further.

Jamal reached the gate, and just as Nasreen had

previously instructed, presented his ticket to the stewardess. She realized immediately that the young man did not understand a word that she was saying, and she took him under her wing. Jamal obediently followed her down the ramp, outdoors to the tarmac, then up the stairs to the plane, where she showed him to his seat. She nodded encouragingly, took the suitcase from his hand, stowed it securely in the overhead compartment, and buckled his seatbelt for him.

The plane belonged to the *British Overseas Airways Corporation*, the company which would later become *British Airways*.

All seatbelts were fastened before the engines came to life, the plane rumbled, and moments later, sped down the runway. Jamal's excitement grew when it lifted off, for never before had he been so high off the ground. He peered out the window, and even though he could not see clearly, he was confident that Nasreen, in the company of friends and family, would be watching the plane until it flew out of sight.

His flight would stop twice before it reached London, England. Jamal would learn much later that the entire distance from Karachi to London was nearly 4,000 miles.

The first stop was a relatively short distance away, at the terminal in Basra, Iraq. Jamal looked on in silence while the plane began to empty. He watched as some people left the plane, and nearly an hour later, new passengers filled their vacant seats.

By the time his plane left Iraq for Berlin, he'd had a long day, and had not yet had a chance to eat. The stewardess seemed to have read his mind, and she approached Jamal with a trolley loaded with cups of liquid. He accepted the cup she offered to him, and this would become his first taste of juice. It was like nothing that he'd ever drank before - he found it delicious and only left him longing for more.

She soon returned with the trolley, this time carrying a variety of food items, all of which were completely foreign to him. She indicated with her hands toward her mouth, and in that way, asked if he was hungry. Jamal nodded eagerly and carefully inspected the snacks that she offered. Nasreen had warned him not to eat any meat while in transit, for he would not be certain which foods may or may not contain pork. As he ate, he looked from the back of the plane to the front, and wondered where the kitchen that produced such food, could possibly be.

Once the plane reached Berlin, all of the passengers were ordered off, to pass through an additional security clearance. Jamal was pulled aside, and told to sit down. The guards demanded to inspect his suitcase, and they motioned for him to open it. Jamal did as he was told, and he was curious as to why they all laughed, for all it contained was a second set of clothes and a pair of shoes. After having his thumbprints taken, he was ordered to re-board the plane.

Jamal's stewardess did not abandon him once they landed at the London Airport (this airport would be renamed, *Heathrow Airport* in 1966). Due to the language barrier, he was unable to express his gratitude as she handed him his suitcase, took him by his free arm, and led him through the busy airport and outside to a waiting taxi.

His layover in London would last two days, and Gafoor's travel arrangements had included his stay at a beautiful hotel. Little did Jamal realize it, but the assistance of the stewardess had also been pre-arranged, and she would dutifully stand by to ensure his safe passage to Canada.

He checked in at the front desk and gazed around in amazement. Until that moment, he did not know that splendid buildings such as this existed. The concierge, an elderly man, motioned for Jamal to follow him up the stairs to the room that would be his home for the next two days. He unlocked the door and stepped aside so Jamal could go in. Just as quickly then, the concierge closed the door behind him, and he was left alone.

Jamal was not sure what he was supposed to do next. A lamp sat brightly lit on the small table next to the bed (he had never seen a raised bed until then), and it was a peculiar thing, as it held no real flame that he could see. He set his suitcase down, moved closer to it, and fiddled with the switch, turning it off, then on, then off again. He was awestruck as he found, then played with a similar switch on the wall that he soon learned, operated a bulb that hung from the ceiling.

Hungry, Jamal left his room to find a place to get something to eat. Not knowing any better, he'd left the door to his room wide open, and walked down the hallway that led back to the staircase. He returned to the lobby, and just as the stewardess had done to him earlier, motioned with his hand to his mouth to the concierge. The man understood what Jamal meant and kindly pointed him in the direction of the dining room.

Jamal found an empty table, sat down, and paid close attention to his surroundings. Everyone was so happy that Jamal could not help but smile. He thought he may have actually arrived in heaven - people were dancing gaily in the next room while a band played interesting music in the background. The men were dressed in military uniforms and their dancing partners wore elegant, floor length gowns.

In the dining room, waiters strode from table to table, carrying trays of full plates to appreciative patrons. Jamal was confused as he did not know how to go about asking for a meal.

After sitting for some time and feeling quite lost, Jamal felt a sharp tap on his shoulder. He turned around, and saw a uniformed man sitting at the next table. To his great relief, the man began to talk in fluent Pashto. He explained that he was a retired colonel from the British Army, and that he had served in Peshawar, Pakistan. Jamal enjoyed speaking with him for a few minutes, before the colonel excused himself and left the table. Jamal watched as the man approached one of the waiters, and returned shortly after with a heaping plate of food and glass of water, which he set down on the table. Jamal thanked him and dug in eagerly, cautiously avoiding anything that could have been pork.

It was late in the evening by the time Jamal would return to his room. As he had seen the colonel do before, he excused himself, left the dining room and walked back toward the staircase.

When he arrived at his room, he noticed that the door was now closed, and he could hear noises originating from inside. Jamal didn't know who was more surprised when he opened it - him, or the man and woman who had found the open room and helped themselves to his bed. They jumped up, straightened their clothes, and may have uttered apologies before they quickly fled the scene. More knowledgeable now, Jamal closed the door behind them. He climbed onto the bed and fell into a deep sleep, without realizing that he was meant to pull the blankets back so he could sleep underneath them.

Two days went by, and during the early morning hours of his final stay in London, he awoke in a panic to an abrupt, constant knocking at his door. He was perplexed - he did not know what this meant, as there was no such thing as door knocking in Charuna.

He rubbed the sleep from his eyes, cautiously approached his door, and opened it. The stewardess stood in the hall, and motioned for him to follow her. He grabbed his suitcase and followed her from his room. Together, they took the taxi back to the airport and he was soon aboard the plane destined for Montreal.

All of his papers were in order and there was no delay going through the customs process; however the line-ups were long, and Jamal nearly missed his flight. The stewardess came to his rescue again, and led him to the departure area. Jamal was anxious - he was now closer than ever to seeing his father at long last.

The plane landed in Vancouver, British Columbia at 3 a.m. on February 14, 1954, and the airport was abuzz with activity. Jamal followed his fellow passengers from the plane, down the stairs to the tarmac. They continued into the airport, down the corridor, to the waiting room, where he found an empty seat. He watched as those that had checked luggage retrieved their bags and left shortly after. He looked on as others were greeted by their loved ones, and then left the room. Jamal was soon the only person remaining, and he wondered where his father was - the sudden silence and stillness in the room had become uncomfortable.

Now that the room was empty, Jamal could distinctly hear a faint whirring noise. The longer he sat in the quiet, the louder the sound became. Curious, he rose from his chair, and followed the whirring until he was confident that he had located the source. He inched his way toward a tall, white metal box, reached out and felt the exterior, noting the slight vibrations. Jamal pulled on the handle - it opened easily, and a gust of cold air rushed out toward him. Alarmed, Jamal jumped back, then quickly closed the door and returned to his seat. That was his first introduction to a refrigerator.

Gafoor was looking for Jamal at the other end of the airport. He'd checked with the airport staff and confirmed that Jamal's flight had arrived on time. It was suggested to him that his son might not have left arrivals. Gafoor promptly waved down a taxicab, and sent the driver to fetch him.

Jamal still did not know what to do or where to go, and his anxiety was getting the best of him. A taxi driver entered the waiting room and called out Jamal's name. Relieved, Jamal followed him out to his car, and climbed into the back seat. The driver steered around to the other side of the building, where despite the hour, many people were standing around. Without a word, he motioned for Jamal to exit his taxicab, and then drove away in search of his next fare.

Jamal, suitcase in hand, stood on the platform and looked around. A man began to walk toward him, although Jamal did not pay him much mind, as his skin was far more fair coloured than his own. Jamal noticed that he was nicely dressed - he wore a suit, hat and long coat.

Gafoor approached the young man that stood off to the side on the platform, and he knew instinctively that this was his son.

"Jamal!" He called out as he neared him. The boy peered closer at Gafoor, and he continued. "I am your father." Jamal could only gape, wide-eyed at his father.

Now that the long awaited moment had arrived, he was speechless. "Stand back and let me look at you." Gafoor watched as his son did as he was told, and his heart burst with pride - the last time he'd seen Jamal, he was a chubby toddler, just two years old. Truly, a slender, tall boy approaching manhood had taken his place. He reached out and embraced his son. "Are you hungry?" The very next day, Gafoor brought his son home.

Gafoor had taken a few days off work to spend time getting to know his son. Just as he'd previously done with Nasreen, he groomed Jamal for life in Canada, and taught him the most basic things that the boy had never before seen nor heard of. Gafoor clearly recalled how he himself had struggled while adapting to this new way of life, and he was keen to pass on all that he had learned to help with the transition.

He was pleased to see that Jamal was eager to learn, and that he quickly picked up on the simple tasks - from learning how to use a toothbrush to eating his meals using utensils, rather than by hand.

Jamal was happy to know that his father was often smiling, and he took delight in hearing him sing the old, familiar Pakhtun folk songs[72], particularly while he'd cook their evening meals.

Two weeks after Jamal's arrival, Gafoor and his son rode the bus to Victoria. They would shop for Jamal's new clothes, and Gafoor would introduce him to a man he held dear to his heart. Jamal had heard all about Sir Robert Holland and everything that he had done for his family, and he looked forward to meeting him.

When Sir Robert Holland answered the knock at his door, Jamal felt as though he was meeting a member of the Royal Family. Sir Robert Holland firmly shook

Jamal's hand in greeting, and nodded his approval to Gafoor.

Not long after, Gafoor introduced Jamal to the foreman at the Youbou sawmill in the hopes of securing a job for his son, but unfortunately, he would not be planning to hire new employees for quite some time. His closing words were hardly discouraging - he suggested that if Jamal were to learn the English language and return in six months' time, he would be hired immediately.

That evening, back at home on Poplar Street, Gafoor translated what the foreman had said, and explained the importance of understanding how to speak the language as well as the significance of literacy to his son. He told him that long before he'd learned how to read and write, he would take letters to his friend that lived in Mesachie Lake, to decipher for him. This conversation reminded Gafoor about another friend, and he and Jamal decided to pay him a visit, to see if he could possibly be of assistance to Jamal.

The Bunker family lived in a sizeable home in nearby Victoria. Theirs was an extremely large family; Mr. and Mrs. Bunker had six sons and five daughters, many of whom were the approximate age of Jamal.

Not only did the Bunkers readily agree to help Jamal learn how to read, write and speak English, but they also graciously welcomed him into their home. It was agreed between the adults that the most effective way for him to learn would be if he were to become part of an English speaking family. Despite Gafoor's repeated offers, they would accept no compensation from him, to support his son while he stayed with them.

On May 2nd, 1955, six months after his first introduction to the foreman, Jamal proudly returned to the Youbou sawmill. The foreman was bewildered as he asked Jamal to write his name down on a piece of paper - Jamal did as he was told. He then produced a newspaper clipping and asked the young man to read it out to him. Again, Jamal obliged him. As promised, he was hired, and began to work on the green chain during the graveyard shift that very night. His starting wage was set at $1.50 per hour, a far cry from the $.42 per hour that Gafoor was earning when he started work at the mill many years before.

Gafoor and Jamal combined their wages and put every single penny they could spare, into the house. Their days off work were spent side by side as they, along with Gafoor's friends, secured the siding onto the exterior walls. Inside, they packed insulation in between the two-by-fours, hung the drywall, installed the flooring and nailed the baseboards in place. Once the second level was ready, Gafoor and Jamal were finally able to move out of the shed. Finishing the main floor would be the next priority on their list of things to do.

While they worked, Gafoor considered all that Jamal had accomplished in the short period of time since he'd arrived. It was evident that Jamal's stay with the Bunker family only seemed to have awakened in him an insatiable appetite for learning - on numerous occasions, Gafoor had found Jamal reading out loud anything he could get his hands on, copying full sentences down, practicing his spelling. Words that he didn't understand or know the meanings of, he'd write down on random slips of paper and bring to work, to inquire with his co-workers as to their definitions.

Gafoor would ensure that his son's education would not stop upon his return to the house on Poplar Street. He hired Mrs. Johnsen, a local teacher who was known for private tutoring, to instruct Jamal in reading and writing for two hours each Sunday. Jamal's penmanship was soon passable, and so he applied for, and was accepted to take courses by correspondence through the Department of Education. Much later, he would earn his Certificate of Achievement for applied English for adults through the Career Institute.

Jamal would read the weekly newspaper, and Gafoor noticed that his son would pay the greatest attention to the advertisements for those searching for world-wide pen pals. Gafoor purchased an Underwood typewriter, and it was not long before Jamal mastered the art of typing. Gafoor was not surprised, when six weeks later, their mailbox was full of correspondence from across the globe - this would continue for the next four years.

One day while they waited for a co-worker to pick them up to drive them to work, out of curiosity, Jamal asked his father why he had not learned to drive, and why he had never bought a vehicle. Gafoor simply replied that in the first place, most of his earnings were sent home to the family, and secondly, any leftover funds went toward the house on Poplar Street. Gafoor had always been more than willing to do without, if it meant that he could provide for his loved ones.

The house was completed in its entirety in 1958 and Gafoor had already applied to sponsor not only his wife and youngest child, Namdar, but also his eldest son, Nasreen, along with his and wife and small children. He was thrilled to know that Nasreen was ready to return to Canada.

As he suspected might be the case, his application was initially rejected, for his financial resources and personal assets were considered minimal and insufficient to sponsor and support six people.

Sir Robert Holland knew exactly how to work around this, and so he prepared separate documents; Jamal would apply to sponsor his mother and Namdar, while Gafoor would apply to sponsor Nasreen and his family. These applications were successful.

At last, after years of struggling and nearly twenty years after Gafoor had first stepped foot on Canadian soil - in 1959 - he was reunited with his family.

AFTERWORD
BY JAMAL KHAN

There really is no crystal ball or any other plausible way of knowing what our fates might have been, had my father had a change of heart, and decided to stay with the ship on November 7th, 1939; but what I believe is this. I believe that to this day, my brothers and I would still be living in the remote village of Charuna at the base of the Hindu Kush mountain range, just north of the Tarbela Dam, on the Indus River. Each of us would have, as our ancestors before us had done, grown up strong, married young, built our stone houses, fathered children, and farmed the land.

As it happened, my brothers and I certainly did grow up strong, and we later married and fathered children – but that is where the similarities end.

I feel grateful to my father every moment of every single day, for the sacrifices he made to provide us with a better way of life. His giving was endless and he asked for nothing in return. I have tried to live my life following the example he set, and if I have achieved this at all - if I have turned out to be half the man he was, when my time comes, I will leave this earth, content.

————

The life that my mother provided for us can hardly be overlooked. During her husband's absence, the weight of maintaining our family and home fell directly upon her shoulders. For twenty years, she was in essence, a single parent - she worked endlessly and without complaint - she was entirely invested in our family, and though she struggled, she succeeded in ensuring that my brothers and I enjoyed our childhoods and experienced a proper upbringing.

————

I also cannot put into words how thankful we are for the friends we've made. So many people helped us along the way; and Sir Robert Holland is just one example - this man was tireless in his crusade to help my father first become a legal immigrant, and later, a Canadian Citizen. Until his passing at the age of 92 in 1965, we made a point of visiting him each year to show our gratitude and respect for all that he'd done for our family.

————

Very much like my father did, I feel privileged to call not one, but two countries that I love deeply - Canada and Pakistan - home. There will always be a special place in my heart for my native land; and due to my father's perseverance, Canada has provided us with opportunities that otherwise would not have been possible.

————

In 1966, I returned to Pakistan to marry the young lady who would become the absolute love of my life. Three years after our wedding, we came back to Canada with our firstborn child, and over the next few years, four more children followed. Gul and I have just celebrated our 50th wedding anniversary and although unrealistic, I would happily spend the next 50 years by her side.

————

My parents have long since passed away, and as per their wishes, they rest together, in the little cemetery located in the village of Charuna.

My mother had fallen ill, and she was taken to the hospital and was being prepared to undergo surgery. I think she had decided that she'd had enough - she closed her eyes peacefully, never to open them again. It was March 25, 1982, and she had lived to see her 76th birthday.

After his wife died, my father had moved in to live with us. One morning as I walked passed his bedroom, I looked in and saw him sitting slumped over on his bed. I asked him if he was all right, and he waved me away.

A few minutes later, I returned to his room to check on him, and I could clearly see that he was not well. I helped him to the car, and we drove off to see the doctor. He took his last breath as he leaned his head on my shoulder. It was December 31, 1983 and he had lived to see his 81st birthday. He had accomplished all that he had set out to do and in my mind, he had reached a level of greatness that few live to see.

In my heart, I know that he died a happy man, and at this moment, he is in heaven, smiling while he sings the old Pashto songs[73] to my mother.

SCRAPBOOK

A collection of
Photographs and Documents
belonging to

JAMAL KHAN

Teresa Schapansky

Photograph copied from the "Original Certificate of Service of Gafoor in the Mercantile Marine", signed by the Shipping Master at the Port of Bombay, dated 1922.

Gafoor Khan - 1940

Basnoor Khan - 1947

Nasreen, Namdar and Jamal (left to right) at Gul
Photography, Rawalpindi, in 1947.
(uncles standing in the background)

Once Gafoor (pictured far right) received the photograph of his children, he arranged to have his photo taken and his image transposed onto their photograph. It was framed and held a place of honour on his bedside table.

Sir Robert Erskine Holland
(date of photograph unknown)

January 30th, 1940

Immigration Officer,
Dominion Immigration Department,
Vancouver, B.C.

Attention of Mr. Taylor.

Dear Sir:-

John Mohmed has worked for this Company
and its predecessor, Industrial Timber Mills Limited, during the
greater part of the last eight years, and is at present in our
employ.

We regard him as a valuable employee, he
being a hardworker and skillful in his duties. He is a teetotler
and a non-smoker, and we understand, a man of some means.

Anything that you can do to regularize
his status so that he can continue to reside in this Country will
be appreciated.

Yours very truly,
BRITISH COLUMBIA FOREST PRODUCTS LIMITED

J.W. Whittaker –
MILL SUPERINTENDENT.

JJ/VGK.

A copy of the letter of support written by Mr.
Whittaker, addressed to the Immigration Officer,
dated January 30th, 1940.

Department of Mines and Resources

IMMIGRATION BRANCH

IN YOUR REPLY REFER TO
NO. 4820-H

PACIFIC DISTRICT SUPERINTENDENT

VANCOUVER, B.C.

March 30,1948

Dear Sir:-

     In connection with your application to remain
in Canada, I would inform you that after carefully reviewing your case, in view of the fact that you are not
admissible to Canada under existing Immigration Regulations,
no action can be taken in this matter and it will be necessary
for you to effect voluntary departure from Canada within sixty
days, failing which it will be necessary for this Department
to effect your deportation.

     Kindly acknowledge receipt of this communication.

Yours truly,

(F.W.Taylor)
District Superintendent

REGISTERED

Gafoor Khan son of Ambersha,
% B.C.Forest Products Ltd.,
595 W.6th Ave.
Vancouver, B.C.

A copy of the letter from the Immigration
Branch advising Gafoor to voluntarily leave
Canada within 60 days, dated March 30, 1948.

CHATEAU LAURIER   April 7, 1948
OTTAWA, ONTARIO

My dear John Mohammed:

    I have just received wires and a letter from Kartar Singh regarding your difficulties and I am indeed sorry to hear of this. The trouble has been that in the first place before I left B. C. I asked Kartar Singh to be sure and let me know when your file and information regarding your case was sent from the Vancouver office to Ottawa. Unfortunately this was not done and your file arrived here without my knowledge and your case was handled by an official, who not knowing the details, merely conformed to the regular immigration rules and confirmed the decision for your deportation made some years ago. When I first enquired about your case some two months ago the department had not received any information concerning you but from my talks with the officials at that time I felt sure that your case could be successfully settled and had I been informed of the arrival of your file I think this would have been so.

    I have already made enquiries about you at the department and today I met several of the immigration officials and I wish to assure you that I shall certainly do everything in my power to see that you do not have to leave the country and I am working hard on the matter now and shall see all the high officials in the department regarding this matter. In the meantime, do not worry unnecessarily and as soon as I have any further news I will let you know right away.

    With kind regard.

      Yours sincerely,

      D. P. Pandia

A copy of the letter addressed to "John Mohammed" from Dr. D.P. Pandia, assuring him that he would work in the background, on his behalf, dated April 7, 1948.

Department of Mines and Resources
IMMIGRATION BRANCH

IN YOUR REPLY REFER TO
NO. 4820-H

PACIFIC DISTRICT SUPERINTENDENT

VANCOUVER, B.C. April 9, 1948.

Dear Sir:-

      Answering your letter of the 3rd instant wherein you ask if you can make a further appeal against the Department's decision with regard to your deportation, may I inform you that your appeal has already been dealt with by the Minister of this Department and unless there was some additional evidence produced I do not see where anything can be gained by further representation.

Yours truly,

F. W. Taylor
District Superintendent.

Gafoor Khan son of Ambersha,
c/o B. C. Forest Products Limited,
Youbou, B. C.

A copy of the letter addressed to Gafoor from Immigration, denying his appeal, dated April 9, 1948.

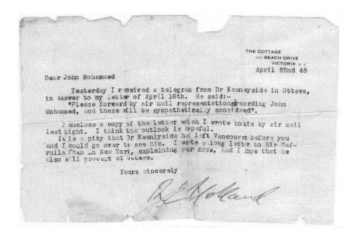

A copy of the letter addressed to "John Mohammed" from Sir Robert Holland, enclosing his letter to Dr. Keenleyside, dated April 22, 1948.

April 21st 48

Dear Dr Keenleyside

I am greatly obliged for your telegram, in reply to my letter of April 16th regarding the case of John Mohammed (Gaffur Khan).

I enclose (Encl I.) a copy of a letter, dated April 18th, from John Mohammed to Mr F.W. Taylor, District Supt, Immigration Branch, Vancouver, begging for an extension of the time-limit of sixty days expiring May 30th, within which he is ordered to depart from Canada. Perhaps this could be taken as his appeal against the order, but if a formal appeal from him is required, I will call him from Youbou and arrange for it to be despatched by air mail.

The facts of his case are no doubt fully stated in yo r records. As I understand them, they are as follows.

John Mohammed arrived on the B.C. coast as a lascar on the P & O ship "Rajputana" about ten years ago, jumped ship, and became an illegal immigrant, as did a good many other illegal immigrants East Indians at the time. He found work in the loggin industry and has been an employee of the B.C. Forest Products Company Ltd, and its predecessor, Industrial Timber Mills Ltd., for the last eight years. I enclose (Encl II.) a copy of a certificate given to him by the Mill Superintendent, Mr Whittaker, and also (Encl III.) a letter written to me by Mr Jeyes, the Chief Accountant of the Company, Cowichan Division. These are strong testimony, in my opinion, to his worthiness and to his ability as an employee.

Dr D.P. Pandia, an eminent Indian from the Madras Province, who has been in Canada for sometime effectively advocating the cause of East Indians in B.C. (and who is now at the Chateau Laurier in Ottawa), suggested to John Mohammed that he shoould endeavour to regularise his position by applying to the Canadian Government for permission to remain in the country. Dr Pandia has, I believe, successfully pleaded the cause of other East Indian 'ill'egal immigrants' and obtained for them the necessary papers.

But unfortunately John Mohammed's application was not successful, and it seems to me possible that, if he had remained in obscurity and not brought his case to notice, nobody would have troubled to dig it up and he could have continued to live his humble and useful life at Youbou. If I am right in this, it may perhaps be regarded as a point in his favor that he voluntarily revealed himself and submitted his petition.

His appeal against the deportation order must rest simply on the fact that, though he entered Canada illegally ten years ago, he had made good and proved himself to be the kind of man that would wreck his life, because he has become thoroughly Canadianised, has forgotten Hindustani, though he remembers his local language, Pashtu, spoken in the Hazar district from which he came; and if he went back, he would find it extremely hard to earn a living as

A copy of the letter addressed to Dr. Keenleyside from Sir Robert Holland, explaining Gafoor's situation in detail, dated April 21, 1948. (page 1 of 2)

a cultivator. He has worked and saved and supported his wife and three children in India in the hope that some day it might be possible for him to get them over to Canada, but even if that is not possible, he wants to be allowed to remain here because he knows that by doing so he can support them in comfort.

The one point which might be considered as prejudicing his claim to remain in Canada is that he is not literate in English. He has a colloquial knowledge of English which serves his need, but he has never been taught and he comes of a thick-headed but honest and faithful peasantry with little aptitude for book-learning. I was in India for thirty years and I can vouch that he comes of good stock and is an honest and worthy man.

I am deeply interested in his case because I know what a tragedy it will be for him if he is forced to leave Canada.

I would gladly vouch for him that he would not disappear into the blue, if the deportation order is stayed pending consideration of his case. What is worrying him at the moment is the fear that he may be seized by the police and held on May 30th in custody pending deportation. If he could be reassured on this point, it would be a great relief to his mind, and he would be able to go on working cheerfully pending the final decision, at all events.

I believe that, if his deportation had to be effected, the C.P.R. have no ships now running to the Orient, nor are they likely to have any for a long time to come. If I am right in this, it would not be a practical possibility to deport John Mohammed for a long while to come, and so it would seem to be the best course to let him continue working where he is for the time being, under guarantee, if required, that he will not try to hide himself.

I have written to Sir Zafrulla Khan, who is, I believe, High Commissioner Designate for Pakistan in Canada, to try to interest him in the case, as John Mohammed's home village is in the Hazara District of Pakistan, and he is of course a Moslem.

I hope very much that the Government may find it possible to stretch the letter of the law a little in John Mohammed's case and include him in the number of 'illegal immigrants' whose position as residents of Canada has, I believe already been regularised.

I will gladly furnish any other information about John Mohammed that may be required.

   With kind regards,

     Yours sincerely

A copy of the letter addressed to Dr. Keenleyside from Sir Robert Holland, explaining Gafoor's situation in detail, dated April 21, 1948. (page 2 of 2)

OFFICE OF THE
DEPUTY MINISTER

CANADA
DEPARTMENT
OF
MINES AND RESOURCES

Ottawa, June 9th, 1948.

Dear Sir Robert:-

        In continuation of my letter dated May 4th, 1948, I am pleased to advise action has now been taken to provide for Gafoor Khan's legal admission to this country by Order-in-Council. The Pacific District Superintendent of Immigration is, therefore, being advised to take the necessary action to grant Gafoor Khan a legal landing in Canada.

        Yours sincerely,

H.L. Keenleyside,
Deputy Minister.

Sir Robert Holland,
The Cottage,
1311 Beach Drive,
Victoria, B.C.

A copy of the letter addressed to Sir Robert Holland indicating that favourable action was being taken on Gafoor's behalf, dated June 9, 1948.

GOVERNMENT OF PAKISTAN

Pakistan House
(SHIPPING DIVISION)
12 East 65th Street
New York 21, N.Y.

TELEPHONE TRAFALGAR 9-5800
CABLE ADDRESS "PAREP"

IN REPLY PLEASE QUOTE FILE NO
SWO-7252-22(55)/50

3rd July, 1950

Dear Sir:

    With reference to your telegram to the Embassy of Pakistan, Washington, D.C. regarding your son M. Nasreen Khan, which was forwarded on to this office, enquiries were made of the United States Immigration and Naturalization Services at Ellis Island, New York, and today we despatched the following telegram to you:

    "US IMMIGRATION ADVISE NASREEN KHAN LEFT NEW YORK SUNDAY EVENING 2nd JULY FOR BRITISH COLUMBIA CANADA"

    Your son was apparently held for verification of departure from New York as he did not possess a visa for the United States.

    I trust that by the time you receive this letter, you will have been reunited with your son.

Yours very truly,

Aftab Ahmad Khan
Vice Consul

Mr. Gafoor Khan,
Empress Hotel,
Vancouver, B.C.
Canada.

KMN

A copy of the letter from New York, explaining the reason for Nasreen's detainment at Ellis Island, dated July 3, 1950.

Teresa Schapansky

CANADA

DEPARTMENT of CITIZENSHIP and IMMIGRATION
MINISTÈRE de la CITOYENNETÉ et de L'IMMIGRATION
IMMIGRATION BRANCH — DIVISION DE L'IMMIGRATION

IN REPLY PLEASE REFER TO
PRIÈRE DE CITER LE DOSSIER

NO. P-4

Victoria, B. C., August 11th 1953.

Gafoor Khan s/o Ambersha,
P.O. Box 510,
Lake Cowichan, B. C.

Dear Sir,

With reference to your application for the entry
to Canada of your son, Jamaul Khan, I wish to advise that our
Head Office wishes to know the present address of Jamaul Khan
and also the present address of your wife and your youngest son
whom you wish to bring forward in 1954.

Your application indicates that the present address
of Jamaul Khan is

c/o Mohd Khan, shopkeeper, Dehri, Hassan Abad,
P.O. Lal Kurti,
Rawalpindi, Pakistan.

Will you kindly advise me if this address is correct and also let
me know the address of your wife and youngest son also.

Will you also let us know how you intend to arrange
for transportation for Jamaul and if Jamaul will be able to report
to our officials at Karachi for examination when he is requested to do
so.

When we have received your reply, the matter will be
continued further.

Yours very truly

J. Dorman
Officer in Charge.

A copy of the letter addressed to Gafoor, in reply to
his application to sponsor Jamal,
dated August 11, 1953.

A copy of Gafoor's long-awaited Certificate of
Canadian Citizenship, dated February 13, 1954.
(Page 1 of 2)

Teresa Schapansky

CERTIFICATE OF CANADIAN CITIZENSHIP

Particulars of Description

Full Name GAFOOR KHAN

Address LAKE COWICHAN, BRITISH COLUMBIA, CANADA

Trade or Occupation MILLWORKER

Place and Date of Birth V. CHARUNA, NORTH WEST FRONTIER
PROVINCE, PAKISTAN
15TH MAY, 1903

Subject of Citizen BRITISH SUBJECT

Married or Single Widower (Widow) Name of Wife Husband MARRIED

Parents Subjects of Citizens GREAT BRITAIN

Age 50 *Years,* *Height* 5 *Feet* 5 *Inches*

Colour BROWN *Complexion* DARK

Colour of Eyes BROWN *Colour of Hair* GRAY

Visible Distinguishing Marks MOLE ON LEFT CHEEK

(COUNTERSIGNED)
REGISTRAR OF CANADIAN CITIZENSHIP

A copy of Gafoor's long-awaited Certificate of
Canadian Citizenship, dated February 13, 1954.
(Page 2 of 2)

128

Jamal Khan - 1965

Teresa Schapansky

Gul Khan - 1967

Photograph taken in 1972, of Jamal
with his friends, Mr. & Mrs. Tommy Douglas
(Mr. Douglas, a fellow immigrant from Scotland,
acted as the Premier of Saskatchewan for 17 years,
became the founding leader of the New Democratic
Party in 1961, and was posthumously voted
"The Greatest Canadian" in 2004).

Last known photograph taken of Gafoor
(with son of Jamal and Gul - Saleem at 8 years old)
dated 1980.

Jamal and Gul's eldest son, Azam at age 17
dated 1986.

Jamal with his dear friend, Miangul Aurangzeb, the last Crown Prince of Swat, dated 2001.

Brothers, Jamal, Namdar and Nasreen (left to right)
dated 2013.

Jamal's collection of pen pal letters and envelopes -
various dates (1956 -1960).

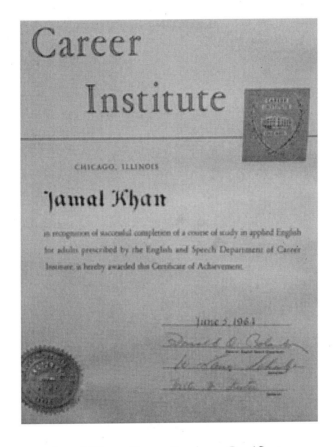

Jamal Khan, Career Institute Certificate
dated 1964.

Teresa Schapansky

Jamal and Gul - 2016

ABOUT THE AUTHOR

(pictured with Jamal Khan)

Teresa Schapansky was introduced to the world of writing at the age of 15, when her word puzzles were accepted for publication in several issues of a television guide. She has written the *Along the Way* (Eye Wonder Studios Inc.) series for young children, as well as two young adult novels, *Imogene of the Pacific Kingdom* (recipient of the Canada Book Award and Readers' Favorite 5 Star Seal), and *Dager of the Tasman Empire* (awarded the Literary Classics Seal of Approval).

Memoirs of a Pakhtun Immigrant is the author's first foray into the world of writing creative non-fiction, and she is currently hard at work on another. The author lives with her family in the Cowichan Valley, on Vancouver Island, British Columbia, Canada.

For more information, please visit:
www.teresaschapansky.com

Teresa Schapansky

BIBLIOGRAPHY

[1]This area lies to the north east of the lush Swat Valley, and formerly known as the ancient Gandhara Region - conquered by Alexander the Great in 327 B.C.: https://www.questia.com/library/journal/1P3-2943416721/alexander-the-great-and-swat

[2] Encyclopaedia Britannica, Indus River: https://www.britannica.com/place/Indus-River

[3]Charuna (also known as Charoona) is located in the Amazai region, in Pakistan: http://amazaionline.com/historyculture/

[4] The North West Frontier Province is the former name of what is now the province, Khyber Pakhtunkhwa, Pakistan. Enclyclopaedia Britannica: https://www.britannica.com/place/Khyber-Pakhtunkhwa

[5] In Pashto, *Maulana*

[6] Often, Pakhtun celebrate the harvesting of crops in a unique fashion: all men from the village gather to harvest the crops in a group while local musicians play in the background. This custom in Pashto, is *ashar*.

[7]Years of Arrests & Imprisonment of Mahatma Gandhi: http://www.mkgandhi.org/arrestofmahatma.htm

[8]Muhammad Ali Jinnah - Biography.com: http://www.biography.com/people/muhammad-ali-jinnah-9354710

[9]BBC History - Mohammad Ali Jinnah (1876-1948): http://www.bbc.co.uk/history/historic_figures/jinnah_mohammad_ali.shtml

[10]The Partition of India by the British: http://thepartitionworldhistory6.weebly.com/jinnah.html

[11]Hayat, Sikandar. *The Charismatic Leader.* Karachi, Pakistan: 2008. Hardcover.

[12]The Canadian Encyclopedia - League of Nations: http://www.thecanadianencyclopedia.ca/en/article/league-of-nations/

[13]Sciences Po - India from 1900 to 1947: http://www.sciencespo.fr/mass-violence-war-massacre-resistance/en/document/india-1900-1947

[14]Encylcopaedia Britannica - The Salt March: <https://www.britannica.com/event/Salt-March>

[15] In Pashto, *nakreezey*

[16] In Pashto, *sandarey*

[17] In Pashto, *tambal*

[18] In Pashto, *dolai*

[19] In Pashto, instruments the likes of *toorai*, *baja*, and *dolkey*

[20] *Ghunsahey* and *darwesh* are traditional Pakhtun delicacies

[21]The Guardian - Mohandas Gandhi's letter to Adolf Hitler, 1939: https://www.theguardian.com/culture/interactive/2013/oct/12/mohandas-gandhi-adolf-hitler-letter

[22]About.com - Muhammad Ali Jinnah: http://asianhistory.about.com/od/pakistan/fl/Muhammad-Ali-Jinnah.htm

[23] Pakistan Defence: http://defence.pk/threads/today-in-1939-entire-congress-party-resigned-mr-jinnah-celeberated.148450/

[24]Ahsan, Aitzen. *The Indus Saga and the Making of Pakistan.* Lahore, Pakistan: Jumhoori Publications, 1998. Paperback.

[25]military.wikia.com - SS Rajputana: http://military.wikia.com/wiki/SS_Rajputana

[26]The History of Paldi, British Columbia: http://www.paldi.ca/?p=1

[27]Wikipedia, The Free Encyclopedia - Continuous Journey Regulation: https://en.wikipedia.org/wiki/Continuous_journey_regulation

[28] Also known as the Pakistan Resolution - http://storyofpakistan.com/lahore-resolution

[29]Hayat, Sikandar. *The Charismatic Leader.* Karachi, Pakistan: 2008. Hardcover.

[30] Story of Pakistan: http://storyofpakistan.com/chaudhry-rehmat-ali

[31]History.com - Pearl Harbor: <http://www.history.com/topics/world-war-ii/pearl-harbor>

[32]A letter from the private collection of documents belonging to Jamal Khan

[33]Wikipedia, The Free Encyclopedia - United Nations: https://en.wikipedia.org/wiki/United_Nations

[34]The Nation - Jinnah as First Governor General of Pakistan: http://nation.com.pk/national/11-Sep-2015/quaid-e-azam-as-first-governor-general-of-pakistan-some-interesting-and-important-events

[35] Shah, Dr. Safdar Ali, and Kazi, Syed Javaid A. Kazi. *The Sikh Heritage of Pakistan.* Lahore, Pakistan, Hardcover.

[36]Insight on Conflict - Kashmir: Conflict Profile: https://www.insightonconflict.org/conflicts/kashmir/conflict-profile/

[37]History of Pakistan Railways in Urdu: http://www.urdumania.net/history-of-pakistan-railways-in-urdu/

[38]Universal Declaration of Human Rights: http://www.un.org/en/universal-declaration-human-rights/

[39]Wikipedia - The Free Encyclopedia - Gandhi Smriti: https://en.wikipedia.org/wiki/Gandhi_Smriti

[40]A letter from the private collection of documents belonging to Jamal Khan

[41]A letter from the private collection of documents belonging to Jamal Khan

[42]A letter from the private collection of documents belonging to Jamal Khan

[43]A letter from the private collection of documents belonging to Jamal Khan

[44]A letter from the private collection of documents belonging to Jamal Khan

[45] Amb no longer exists. The construction of the Tarbela dam (beginning in 1968) led to the loss of 135 villages and the displacement of about 96,000 people: https://en.wikipedia.org/wiki/Tarbela_Dam

[46]CP - Our History http://www.cpr.ca/en/about-cp/our-history

[47] Wikipedia, the Free Encyclopedia - Canadian Pacific Railway Coast Service: https://en.wikipedia.org/wiki/Canadian_Pacific_Railway_Coast_Service

[48]Dawn.com, The foreign policy of Liaquat Ali Khan: http://www.dawn.com/news/881096

[49] Story of Pakistan - Liaquat Ali Khan: http://storyofpakistan.com/liaquat-ali-khan/

[50]Encyclopaedia Brittanica - Liaquat Ali Khan: https://www.britannica.com/biography/Liaquat-Ali-Khan

[51]History Pak - Liaquat-Nehru Pact: http://historypak.com/liaquat-nehru-pact/

[52] The city of Abbottabad is well known as being the home of the Pakistan Military Academy

[53] Karachi is the former capital city of Pakistan: http://pakistanpaedia.com/isb/islamabad.html

[54] A letter from the private collection of documents belonging to Jamal Khan

[55] CBC News - Princess Elizabeth's 1951 Royal Visit to Canada: http://www.cbc.ca/news/world/princess-elizabeth-s-1951-royal-visit-to-canada-1.1061794

[56] Canada's History - Un-forgetting the Korean War: http://www.canadashistory.ca/Magazine/Online-Extension/Articles/Un-forgetting-the-Korean-War

[57] Wikipedia - The Free Encyclopedia - The Pakistani nationality law: https://en.wikipedia.org/wiki/Pakistani_nationality_law

[58] Wikipedia - The Free Encyclopedia - Liaquat Ali Khan, Assassination: https://en.wikipedia.org/wiki/Liaquat_Ali_Khan#Assassination

[59] Historypak.com: http://historypak.com/liaquat-ali-khan/

[60] Dawn.com: The First Lady: http://www.dawn.com/news/785779

[61] Wikipedia, The Free Encyclopedia - Ra'ana Liaquat Ali Khan: https://en.wikipedia.org/wiki/Ra%27ana_Liaquat_Ali_Khan

[62] Islamabad is the current capital city of Pakistan: Encyclopaedia Britannica: https://www.britannica.com/place/Islamabad

[63] Pakistan Academy of Sciences: http://www.paspk.org/introduction-to-the-academy/

[64]Wikipedia, The Free Encyclopedia - Coronation of Queen Elizabeth II: https://en.wikipedia.org/wiki/Coronation_of_Queen_Elizabeth_II

[65]Wikipedia, The Free Encylcopedia - Benazir Bhutto: https://en.wikipedia.org/wiki/Benazir_Bhutto

[66]Native Pakistan Role Models: http://nativepakistan.com/role-models/

[67] Encyclopaedia Britannica - Hindu Kush: https://www.britannica.com/place/Hindu-Kush

[68] Wikipedia, The Free Encyclopedia - Nanga Parbat: https://en.wikipedia.org/wiki/Nanga_Parbat#First_ascent

[69] digplanet - Qaumi Taranah: http://www.digplanet.com/wiki/Qaumi_Taranah

[70] In Pashto, *numberdar*

[71]Wikipedia, The Free Encyclopedia - Aga Khan III: https://en.wikipedia.org/wiki/Aga_Khan_III

[72] In Pashto, *tappey*

[73]Gafoor took great delight in listening to and singing the songs written by the famous 16th century poet, Rahman Baba: https://learnpashto.wordpress.com/category/poetry-of-rehman-baba/